PURITAN PAPERBACKS

The Glorious Feast of the Gospel

D1557840

Richard Sibbes

1577–1635

'Of this blest man, let this just praise be given: heaven
was in him, before he was in heaven.' So wrote Izaak
Walton of Richard Sibbes, lecturer at Holy Trinity,
Cambridge, 1610–15; preacher at Gray's Inn, London,
from 1616; master of Catherine Hall, Cambridge, from
1626 to his death in 1635. After William Perkins, the
'heavenly' Dr Sibbes was the most significant of the
great Puritan preachers of Cambridge, and his writings show the reason why. Strong thoughts, simple
sentences, deep knowledge of the Bible and the human
heart, and a sure pastoral touch, are here revealed in a
sustained concentration on the glory and grace of God
in Christ.

Known in his day as 'the sweet dropper' because of
the confidence and joy to which his sermons gave rise,
Sibbes concentrated on exploring the love, power and
patience of Christ, and the riches of the promises of
God. He was a pioneer in working out the devotional
application of the doctrine of God's covenant grace.

There is no better introduction to the Puritans than
the writings of Richard Sibbes, who is, in many ways,
a typical Puritan. 'Sibbes never wastes the student's
time,' wrote C. H. Spurgeon, 'he scatters pearls and
diamonds with both hands.'

Richard Sibbes

The Glorious Feast of the Gospel

or

Christ's Gracious Invitation
and
Royal Entertainment of Believers

THE BANNER OF TRUTH TRUST

THE BANNER OF TRUTH TRUST

Head Office
3 Murrayfield Road
Edinburgh, EH12 6EL
UK

North America Office
PO Box 621
Carlisle, PA 17013
USA

banneroftruth.org

First published 1650
The text of this volume is based on
Alexander B. Grosart's edition of the
Works of Richard Sibbes, 7 vols (1862–64), vol 2

© The Banner of Truth Trust 2021
*

ISBN
Print: 978 1 80040 090 0
Epub: 978 1 80040 091 7
Kindle: 978 1 80040 092 4
*

Typeset in 10/13 Minion Pro at
The Banner of Truth Trust, Edinburgh

Printed in the USA by
Versa Press Inc.,
East Peoria, IL

Contents

To the Reader

So much of late hath been written about the times, that spiritual discourses are now almost out of season. Men's minds are so hurried up and down, that it is to be feared they are much discomposed to think seriously as they ought, of their eternal concernments. Alas! Christians have lost much of their communion with Christ and his saints – the heaven upon earth – whilst they have wofully disputed away and dispirited the life of religion and the power of godliness, into dry and sapless controversies about government of church and state. To recover therefore thy spiritual relish of savoury practical truths, these sermons of that excellent man of God, of precious memory, are published. Wherein thou art presented.

I. An admirable feast indeed; wherein Jesus Christ, the eternal Son of God, is the bridegroom, where every believer that hath 'put on' the Lord Jesus, Rom. 13:14, 'the wedding garment,' Matt. 22:11, is not only the guest, but the spouse of Christ, and the bride at this wedding supper. Here Jesus Christ is the master of the feast, and the cheer and provision too. He is the 'Lamb of God,' John 1:29, the 'ram caught in the thicket,' Gen. 22:13. He is the 'fatted calf,' Luke 15:23. When he was sacrificed, 'wisdom killed her beasts,'

Prov. 9:2. At his death, 'the oxen and fatlings were killed,' Matt. 22:4. Ἀληθῶς βρῶσις και ἀληθῶς πόσις (*Alēthōs brōsis kai alēthōs posis*). His 'flesh is meat indeed, and his blood is drink indeed,' John 6:55. And that thou mayest be fully delighted at this feast, Christ is the 'rose of Sharon,' the 'lily of the valley,' Song of Song 2:1. He is a 'bundle of myrrh,' Song of Sol. 1:13, a 'cluster of camphire,' Song of Sol. 1:14; his name is 'an ointment poured out,' Song of Sol. 1:3, and 'his love is better than wine,' Song of Sol. 1:2. In Christ are 'all things ready,' Matt. 22:4, for 'Christ is all in all,' Col. 3:11. And great is the feast that Christ makes for believers, for it is the marriage feast which the great King 'makes for his Son,' Matt. 22:2; the great design and aim of the gospel being to exalt the Lord Jesus Christ, and give 'him a name above every name,' Philip. 2:10. Great is the company that are bid, Luke 14:16, Jews and Gentiles. God keeps open house, 'Ho, every one that thirsteth, come,' Isa 55:1, and 'whosoever will, let him come, and freely take of the water of life,' Rev. 22:17. Great is the cheer that is provided. Every guest here hath Asher's portion, 'royal dainties and bread of fatness,' Gen. 49:20. Here is all excellent best wine, 'wine upon the lees well refined,' Isa. 25:6. Here is 'fat things,' yea, 'fat things full of marrow,' Rev. 2:17, the 'water of life,' Rev. 22:17, and the fruit of 'the tree of life which is in the midst of the paradise of God,' Gen. 2:9. All that is at this feast is of the best, yea, the best of the best. Here is variety and plenty too. Here is 'bread enough and to spare.' The feasts of Caligula and Heliogabalus, who ransacked the earth, air, and sea to furnish their tables, were nothing to this. And above all, here is welcome for every hungry, thirsty soul. *Super omnia vultus accessere boni.*[1] He that bids thee come, will bid thee welcome. He will not say eat when his heart is not with thee. The invitation is free, the preparation great, and the entertainment at this feast – suiting the magnificence of the great King – is full and bountiful. All which is at large treated of in these excellent sermons, which are therefore deservedly entitled, 'The marriage Feast between Christ and his Church.' We read of a philosopher that, having prepared an excellent treatise of happiness, and presenting it unto a great king, the king answered him, 'Keep your book to yourself, I am not now at leisure.'[2] Here is an excellent treasure put into thy hand; do not answer us, I am not now at leisure. Oh, do not let Christ stand 'knocking at thy heart, who will come and sup with thee,' Rev. 3:20, and bring his cheer with him. Oh, let not a 'deceived heart turn thee any longer aside to feed upon ashes,' Isa. 44:20; feed no longer with swine 'upon husks,' Luke 15:16, while thou mayest be filled and satisfied 'with bread in thy father's house,' Luke 15:17.

But this is not all; if thou wilt be pleased to peruse this book, thou wilt find there are many other useful, seasonable, and excellent subjects handled besides the marriage-feast.

II. Jesus Christ hath not only provided a feast, but because he is desirous that all those for whom it is provided should come to it (which only they do that believe), *he takes*

---

[1] Latin: 'above all friendly expressions were added.' This is taken from Ovid's *Metamorphoses*.

[2] 'Keep your book to yourself.' Thomas Brooks in his 'Epistle Dedicatory' to his *Apples of Gold*, thus introduces the anecdote. 'I hope none of you, into whose hands it may fall, will say as once Antipater, King of Macedonia, did, when one presented him with a book teaching of happiness. His answer was οὐ σχολάζω (*ou scholazo*), "I have no leisure."'

away the veil of ignorance and unbelief from off their hearts; and here you shall find this skilful preacher hath excellently discoursed what this veil is, how it naturally lies upon all, and is only removed by the Spirit of Christ. And if the Lord hath 'destroyed this covering from off thy heart,' we doubt not, but the truth of this heavenly doctrine will shine comfortably into thy soul.

III. Jesus Christ, to make his bounty and mercy further appear in this feast, *he hath given his guests the 'bread of life,' and hath secured them from the fear of death.* They need not fear. There is no *mors in ollâ*[3] at this feast. We may feast without fear. Jesus Christ by his 'tasting of death hath swallowed it up in victory,' 1 Cor. 15:54. Christ doth not make his people such a feast as it is reported Dionysius the tyrant once made for his flatterer Damocles, who set him at a princely table, but hanged a drawn sword in a small thread over his head.[4] But Christ would have us triumph over the king of fears, who was slain by the death of Christ, and we thereby delivered from the bondage of the fear of death, Heb. 2:14, 15.

At other feasts they were wont of old to have a death's head served in amongst other dishes, to mind them in the midst of all their mirth of their mortality (which practice of the heathens condemns the ranting jollity of some loose professors in these times). *Κατῆλθεν εἰς θάνατον ἀθάνατος, και τῷ θάνατῳ καθεῖλε θάνατον* (*Katēlthen eis thanaton athanatos, kai tō thanatō katheile thanaton*). But here,

[3] Latin: 'death in the pot,' cf. 2 Kings 4:40.
[4] For this well-known anecdote, consult Cicero (Tusc. v. 21.), and Horace (Carm. iii., 1. 17).

Christ serves in death's head, as David 'the head of Goliath,' 1 Sam. 17:54, the head of a slain and conquered death. Our Samson by his own death 'hath destroyed death, and hath thereby ransomed us from the hand of the grave, and hath redeemed us from death,' Hos. 13:14, and the slavish fear of it. All which is at large handled in these following sermons for thy comfort and joy, that thou mayest triumph in his love, through whom thou art more than conqueror.

IV. Because 'it is a merry heart that makes a continual feast,' Prov. 15:15, and that this feast might be a gaudy-day[5] indeed unto thy soul, Christ doth here promise, 'to wipe away all tears from off the faces of his people,' Isa. 25:8. The gospel hath comforts enough to make glad the hearts of the saints and people of God. The 'light of God's countenance' will refresh them with 'joy unspeakable and glorious,' 1 Pet. 1:8, in the midst 'of the valley of the shadow of death,' Psa. 23:4. A truly godly person can weep for his sins, though the world smile never so much upon him; and though he be never so much afflicted in the world, yet he can and will 'rejoice in the God of his salvation,' Hab. 3:18. In these sermons thou hast this gospel-promise sweetly opened and applied; wherein thou shalt find directions when, and for what, to mourn and weep, and the blessedness of all true mourners, 'whose sorrow shall be turned into joy,' John 16:20.

V. In these sermons you shall further find, *that though Jesus Christ respect his people highly, and entertain them bountifully, yet they have but coarse usage in the world*, who

---

[5] That is, a 'day of rejoicing.'

are wont to revile them as 'fools' and 'mad men,' as 'seditious rebels,' 'troublers of Israel,' 'proud and hypocritical persons.' But blessed are they that do not 'stumble at this stone of offence,' Rom. 9:32, that wear the 'reproaches of Christ as their crown,' and by 'well-doing put to silence the ignorance of foolish men,' 1 Pet. 2:15; for let the world load them with all their revilings, yet 'the spirit of glory rests upon them,' 2 Cor. 12:9, and in due time he will roll away their reproach, 'and bring forth their judgment as the light, and their righteousness as the noon-day,' Psa. 37:6.

VI. And because a Christian here hath more in hope than in hand, more in reversion than in possession, 'walks by faith' rather than sense, and 'lives by the word of God, and not by bread alone,' Matt. 4:4, thou shalt have here, Christian reader, a sweet discourse *of the precious promises of Christ* which he hath left us here to stay the stomach of the soul, till we come to that feast of feasts in heaven; that by this glimpse we might in part know the 'greatness of that glory which shall be revealed,' 1 Peter 5:1; that the first-fruits might be a pawn of the harvest, and the 'earnest of the Spirit,' Eph. 1:14, a pledge of that full reward we shall have in heaven, where we shall be brimful of those 'pleasures that are at God's right hand forever,' Psa. 16:11. Christ hath given us promises to uphold our faith and hope, till faith be perfected in fruition, and hope end in vision, till Jesus Christ, who is here the object of our faith, be the reward of our faith forever.

VII. Now because the comfort of the promises is grounded in the faithfulness of him that hath promised, this godly and learned man hath strongly asserted *the divine authority of the holy Scriptures*, proving that they are θεόπνευστοι (*theoneustoi*), that they are the very word of God, that they are αὐτόπιστοι (*autopistoi*) and ἀξόπistoi (*axopistoi*), worthy of all acceptation, and belief, for their own sakes; a truth very seasonable for these times, to antidote thee against the poisonfull errors of blasphemous anti-scripturists.

VIII. Lastly, because that God often takes a long day for performance of the promise, thou shalt find herein the doctrine of *waiting upon God*, excellently handled; a duty which we earnestly commend unto thy practice, as suitable to these sad times. Say, O say with the church, 'In the way of thy judgments, O Lord, we have waited for thee,' Isa. 26:8; and with the prophet, 'I will wait upon the Lord that hideth his face from the house of Jacob, and I will look for him,' Isa. 8:17. And rest assured, that 'none of the seed of Jacob shall seek him in vain,' Isa. 45:19; he will not 'disappoint their hope, nor make their faces ashamed that wait for him,' Isa. 49:23.

Thus we have given you a short prospect of the whole, a brief sum of that treasure which these sermons contain. We need say nothing of the author; his former labours 'sufficiently speak for him in the gates,' Prov. 31:23; his memory is highly honoured amongst the godly-learned. He that enjoys the glory of heaven, needs not the praises of men upon earth. If any should doubt of these sermons, as if they should not be truly his, whose name they bear, let him but observe the style, and the excellent and spiritual matter herein contained, and he will, we hope, be fully satisfied. Besides, there are many ear-witnesses yet living, who can clear them from any shadow of imposture. They come forth without any alteration, save only some repetitions (which the pulpit did well bear) are here omitted.

The Lord make these, and all other the labours of his servants, profitable to his church. And the Lord so 'destroy the veil' from off thy heart, that thou mayest believe, and by faith come to this feast, the joy and comfort whereof may swallow up all the slavish fear of death, dry up thy tears, and roll away all reproach. And the Lord give thee a waiting heart, to stay thy soul upon the name of the Lord, to believe his word, and his faithful promises, that in due time thou mayest 'rejoice in the God of thy salvation.' This is the earnest prayer of

ARTHUR JACKSON.

JAMES NALTON.

WILL TAYLOR.[4]

LONDON, *April* 19, 1650.

⁶ Arthur Jackson, like Sibbes, was a native of Suffolk, having been born at Little Waldingfield, in 1593. He won the respect of even Laud. It is told that when the *Book of Sports* was commanded to be publicly read, he refused compliance, and was complained of for his contumacy to the Archbishop, but that prelate would not suffer him to be molested. 'Mr Jackson,' said he, 'is a quiet and peaceable man, and therefore I will not have him meddled with.' Sheldon manifested like esteem for him. At the Restoration, when Charles II made his entrance into the city, Jackson was appointed by his brethren to present to him a Bible, as he passed through St Paul's Churchyard, which was in his parish; when he addressed the king in a congratulatory speech, which was graciously received. He was also one of the Commissioners of the Savoy. He

died, Aug. 5, 1666, one of the most venerable of the 'ejected' two thousand. Consult *Nonconformist's Memorial*, vol. i. pp. 120-124; also 'Memoir' prefixed to his *Annotations*, vol. iv.

James Nalton. This 'man of God,' beloved by Richard Baxter, and all his like-minded contemporaries, was called 'The Weeping Prophet,' because of his peculiarly tender and tearful nature. He also was one of the 'two thousand,' but died shortly afterwards in 1663. In a copy of Sedgwick's *Bowels of Tender Mercy Sealed in the Everlasting Covenant* (folio 1661), in our possession, is the following inscription, 'Mary Nalton, her book, given by her dear husband, Ja. Nalton, Sept. 14, 1661.' Consult *Noncf. Mem.*, vol. i. pp. 142-144.

This 'William Taylor,' was probably the author of a sermon in the *Morning Exercises*, and the same for whom Dr Spurstowe preached a remarkable funeral sermon. He died in 1661. – G.

GLORIOUS FEAST

OF THE

GOSPEL

OR,

Christ's gracious Invitation and royall
Entertainment of Believers.
Wherein amongst other things these comfortable
Doctrines are spiritually handled:

Viz:

1. *The Marriage Feast between Christ and his Church.*
2. *The vaile of Ignorance and Vnbeliefe removed.*
3. *Christ's Conquest over death.*
4. *The wiping away of teares from the faces of God's people.*
5. *The taking away of their Reproaches.*
6. *The precious Promises of God, and their certaine performance.*
7. *The Divine Authority of the Holy Scriptures.*
8. *The Duty and comfort of waiting upon God.*

Delivered in divers Sermons upon Isa. 25:6-9,

by

The late Reverend, Learned and faithfull Minister of the Gospell,
RICHARD SIBBS, D.D. Master of *Katherine*-Hall in *Cambridge*,
and Preacher at Grayes-Inn, *London.*

Prov. 9:1-5.

The Marriage Feast between Christ and His Church

Sermon 1

In this mountain shall the Lord of hosts make unto all people a feast of fat things, a feast of wines on the lees; of fat things full of marrow, of wine on the lees well refined.
— Isaiah 25:6

In the former chapter the holy prophet having spoken of the miseries and desolation of the church, in many heavy, sad, and doleful expressions; as 'the vine languisheth, the earth is defiled under the inhabitants thereof, because they have transgressed the laws, changed the ordinance, and broken the everlasting covenant; therefore the earth shall be accursed, and they that dwell therein shall not drink wine with a song,' etc. Here you see all sweetness and rejoicing of heart is departed from them; yet even in the midst of all these miseries, God, the God of comforts, makes sweet and gracious promises to his church, to raise it out of its mournful estate and condition. And therefore the prophet, in the former part of this chapter, speaks of blessing God for the destruction of his enemies, and for his great love to his church. And when he had spoken of the ruin of the enemy, he presently breaks out with thanksgiving, breathing forth abundant praises to his God; as it is the custom of holy men, guided by the motion of the blessed Spirit of God, upon all occasions, but especially for benefits to his church, to praise his name, not out of ill affection at the destruction of the adversaries, but at the execution of divine justice, for the fulfilling of the truth of his promise; as in the first verse of this chapter, 'O Lord, thou art my God; I will exalt thee, I will praise thy name; for thou hast done wonderful things; thy counsels of old are faithfulness and truth.' When the things that were promised of old were brought to pass, the church was ever ready to give God the glory of his truth. Therefore, rejoice not when thine enemies fall; but when the enemies of the Lord are brought to desolation, then we may, nay, we ought to sing, 'Hallelujah' to him that liveth forever and ever.

I will now fall upon the very words of my text. 'In this mountain shall the Lord of hosts make unto all people a feast of fat things,' etc. These words they are prophetical, and cannot have a perfect performance all at once, but they shall be performed gradually. The promise of 'a new heaven and a new earth,' 2 Pet. 3:13, shall be performed. The conversion of the Jews, and the bringing in of the fulness of the Gentiles, shall gradually be brought to pass. All the promises that ever God hath made, before the second coming of Christ to judgment, shall be accomplished. God hath made his peace with us in the gospel of peace; and when all these promises shall be fulfilled, then all imperfection shall be done away, and we shall never be removed from our Rock; but our joy shall then be full. Nay, even in this life we have some degrees of perfection. We have grace, and the means of grace; the ordinances of Christ, and a testimony of everlasting glory.

'*In this mountain will the Lord of hosts make a feast.*'

In these words ye have set down a glorious and a royal feast; and the *place* where this feast is to be kept is 'Mount Zion'; the *feast-maker* is 'the Lord of hosts'; the *parties invited*, are 'all people'; *the issues of it, and the provision* for the feast, are 'fat things,' and 'wine' of the best; a feast of the best of the best, a feast of the fat and of the marrow, a feast of 'wine on the lees well refined.'

Here you may see that God doth veil heavenly things under earthly things, and condescends so low as to enter into the inward man by the outward man. For our apprehensions are so weak and narrow, that we cannot be acquainted with spiritual things, but by the inward working of the Spirit of the Almighty.

This 'mountain' is *the place* where this feast is made, even 'mount Zion'; which is a type and figure of the church, called in Scripture, 'the holy mountain.' For as mountains are raised high above the earth, so the church of God is raised in excellency and dignity above all the sorts of mankind.

Observation. 1. *As much as men above beasts, so much is the church raised above all men.* This mountain is above all mountains. The 'mountain of the Lord' is above all mountains whatsoever. 'Thou, O mountain, shalt stand immoveable,' when all other mountains shall smoke, if they are but touched. This is the mountain of mountains. The church of God is most excellent in glory and dignity, as ye may see in the latter end of the former chapter, how the glory of the church puts down all other glories whatsoever.

[3]

'The moon,' saith the prophet, 'shall be confounded, and the sun ashamed, when the Lord of hosts shall reign in Mount Zion, and in Jerusalem, and before his ancients gloriously.' So that the brightness of the church shall put down the glory of the sun and of the moon. Thus you see the church of God is a mountain.

Reason. First, *Because God hath established it upon a stronger foundation than all the world besides.* It is founded upon the goodness and power and truth of God. Mountains of brass and iron are not so firm as this mountain. For what sustains the church but the word of God? And being built upon his word and truth, it may very well be called a mountain, for it shall be as mount Zion, which shall never be removed, Psa. 125:1. It may be moved, but never removed. Thus, in regard to the firmness and stability thereof, it may rightly be termed a mountain.

Observation. 2. Again, *we may here speak in some sort of the visibility of the church.* But here will arise a quarrel for the papists, who when they hear of this mount, they presently allude[1] it to their church. Their church, say they, is a mount; so saith the Scripture.

I answer, *Firstly,* We confess in some sort their church to be a mount (though not this mount), for Babylon is built on seven hills; but if this prove her a church, it is an antichristian church. *Secondly,* That the Catholic Protestantial[2] church had always a being, though sometimes invisible. The apostle, writing to the Romans, exhorts them 'not to be high minded, but fear'; for, saith he, 'if God hath broken

---

[1] That is, = 'make it refer to.'
[2] That is, 'Protestant.'

off the natural branches, perhaps he will break off you also,' Rom. 11:21, 24. And, indeed, for their pride and haughtiness of mind, they are at this day broken off. Christ, that 'walks between the seven golden candlesticks,' Rev. 2:1, did never say that the church of Smyrna or Ephesus should always remain a visible church to the eyes of the world, neither were they; for to this very day they lie under bondage and slavery to the Turk. The mount hath been always visible, though not always alike gloriously visible. For there will be a time when the church shall fly into the wilderness, Rev. 12:6. Where, then, shall be the glorious visibility of the church? There is a time when all shall follow the beast. The papists themselves confess that in antichrist's time the church shall scarce be visible. The essence of a thing and the quality of a thing may differ. The church is a church, and visible, but not always equally, and alike gloriously visible; yet those that had spiritual eyes, and did look upon things with the spectacles of the Scripture, they could always declare the church was visible; for, from the beginning of the world, the church had always lustre enough sufficient to delight, and draw the elect, and so shall have to the end of the world, though sometimes the church may have a mist before it, as Augustine speaks: 'It is no wonder that thou canst not see a mountain, for thou hast no eyes.' But the papists have seen this mountain. As they have always been bloody persecutors of the church, they have seen enough to confound them. For we have nothing in our church, but they have the same; only ours is refined, and freed from idolatry. We have two sacraments, they have seven. We have Scripture, they have traditions, which they equal with it. We have Scriptures pure, they, corrupt. So that our church was

[5]

in the midst of theirs, as a sound and more uncorrupt part in a corrupt body.

This mountain is the church. 'The Lamb standeth upon mount Zion, and with him a hundred forty and four thousand, having his Father's name written in their foreheads,' Rev. 14:1. Christ standeth in the church, and standing in mount Zion he is accompanied with those that his Father hath given to him before the world was. Therefore those that belong to this holy mountain, they are Christ's. 'And in this mountain shall the Lord of hosts make a feast for all people.' And this feast is a royal feast, a marriage feast, wherein the joy and comfort of God's people are set down by that which is most comfortable among men. *The founder of the feast* is 'the Lord of hosts.' It is only he that is able to prepare a table in the wilderness, that is mighty and of ability to feast his church with a spiritual and holy banquet. We all live at his table for the feeding of our bodies, but much more in regard of our souls. He can make a feast for the whole man, for he is Lord of the conscience; and he is to spread a table for the whole world. Nay, more, if there were so many, he can furnish a table for ten thousand worlds. He is the God of all spiritual comforts, and the 'God of all consolation.' He is infinite, and can never be drawn dry, for he is the fountain of eternal life. All graces and comforts in the Scripture are called the comforts and graces of the Holy Spirit, because God is the giver of them by his Spirit. Who can take away the wound of a guilty conscience, but he that hath set the conscience in the hearts of men? He, if he pleaseth, can take away the burden of a grieved conscience, and supply it, instead thereof, with new and solid comforts. He knoweth all the windings and turnings of the soul, where all the pain and grief lieth; and he cannot but know it, because he only is above the soul. He is therefore the fittest to make the soul a feast. He only can do it, and he will do it.

'*In this mountain shall the Lord of hosts make a feast.*'
Why is he called the 'Lord of hosts'?
It is an usual term to set forth the glory of God, to make his power and the greatness of his majesty known amongst the children of men.

'*He shall make a feast for all people.*'
Those that are invited to this glorious feast are 'all people.' None excepted, none excluded, that will come to Christ! Some of all sorts, of all nations, of all languages! This hath relation to the time of the gospel. The church at first had its being in particular families, but afterwards more enlarged. The church at the first was of the daughters of men, and the sons of God. The children of the church mingled with a generation of corrupt persons, that would keep in no bounds; but after Abraham's time there was another generation of the church, that so it was a little more enlarged. Then there was a third generation, a divided generation, consisting of Jews and Gentiles. So that, when Christ came into the world, the bounds of the church began to enlarge themselves more and more, so that now it is in this happy condition, 'Come ye all unto me,' all that are heavy laden,' Matt. 11:28. Both Jews and Gentiles, all are invited, whosoever they are, 'nothing is now unclean,' Acts 10:15. Christ is come, and hath made 'to all people a feast of fat things.' It must be a feast, and of fat things, for all the world shall be the better for it. The Jews shall be converted, and the fulness

of the Gentiles shall come in. And yet it is no prejudice to any particular man, because the things ye are to taste of are spiritual. Go to all the good things in the world: the more one hath of them the less another must have, because they are earthly, and so are finite. But in spiritual things all may have the whole, and every man in particular. Every man enjoyeth the light of the sun in particular, and all enjoy it too. So the whole church, and only the church, enjoys the benefit and comfort of this feast; but under the name of this church come all the elect, both 'Jews and Gentiles,' and therefore it must be the Lord of hosts that can make such a feast as this is, a feast for all people. No other is able to do it.

This feast is 'a feast of fat things, full of marrow and of wine on the lees well refined,' *the best that can be imagined, the best of the best*. A feast is promised, a spiritual feast. The special graces and favours of God are compared to a feast made up of the best things, full of all varieties and excellencies, and the chief dish that is all in all, is Christ, and all the gracious benefits we by promise can in any wise expect from him. All other favours and blessings, whatsoever they are, are but Christ dished out, as I may speak, in several offices and attributes. He is the original of comfort, the principle of grace and holiness. All is included in Christ. Ask of him and ye shall obtain, even the forgiveness of your sins, peace of conscience, and communion of saints. Ask of Christ, as of one invested with all privileges for the good of others. But yet this is by his death. He is the feast itself. He is dished out into promises. Have you a promise of the pardon of sins? It is from Christ. Wouldst thou have peace of conscience? It is from Christ. Justification and redemption? It is from Christ. The love of God is derived to us by

Christ, yea, and all that we have that is good is but Christ parcelled out.

Now, I will shew why Christ, with his benefits, prerogatives, graces, and comforts, is compared to a feast.

First. In regard *of the choice of the things.* In a feast all things are of the best; so are the things we have in Christ. Whatsoever favours we have by Christ, they are choice ones. They are the best of every thing. Pardon for sin is a pardon of pardons. The title we have for heaven, through him, is a sure title. The joy we have by him is the joy of all joys. The liberty and freedom from sin, which he purchased for us by his death, is perfect freedom. The riches of grace we have by him are the only lasting and durable riches. Take anything that you can, if we have it by Christ, it is of the best. All worldly excellencies and honours are but mere shadows to the high excellencies and honour we have in Christ. No joy, no comfort, no peace, no riches, no inheritance to be compared with the joy, peace, and inheritance which we have in Christ. Whatsoever we have by him, we have it in a glorious manner. And therefore he is compared to fat, to 'fat things full of marrow,' 'to wine, to wine on the lees,' that preserveth the freshness of it; the best wine of all, that is not changed from vessel to vessel, but keepeth its strength. And, indeed, the strength and vigour of all floweth from Jesus Christ in covenant with us.

The love of Christ is the best love, and he himself incomparably the best, and hath favours and blessings of the choicest.

Second. Again, as in a feast, besides choice, *there is variety*, so in Christ there is variety answerable to all our wants. Are we foolish? He is wisdom. Have we guilt in our consciences? He is righteousness, and this righteousness is imputed unto us. Are we defiled? He is sanctification. Are we in misery? He is our redemption. If there be a thousand kinds of evils in us, there is a thousand ways to remedy them by Jesus Christ. Therefore, the good things we have by Christ are compared to all the benefits we have in this world. In Christ is choice and variety. Are we weak? He is meat to feed us, that we may be strong. He will refresh us. He is the best of meats. He is marrow. So, are our spirits faint? He is wine. Thus we have in Christ to supply all our wants. He is variety. There is a plant among the Indians called by the name of *coquus*;[1] the fruit thereof serveth for meat and drink, to comfort and refresh the body. It yieldeth that whereof the people make apparel to clothe themselves withal, and also that which is physical,[2] very good against the distempers of the body. And if God will infuse so much virtue into a poor plant, what virtue may we expect to be in Christ himself? He feedeth our souls to all eternity, puts upon us the robes of righteousness, heals the distempers of our souls. There is variety in him for all our wants whatsoever. He is food, physic, and apparel to clothe us; and when we are clothed with him, we may with boldness stand before the majesty of God. He is all in all. He is variety, and all. There is something in Christ answerable to all the necessities of God's people, and not only so, but to their full content in everything.

[1] That is, 'cocoa.'
[2] That is, 'medicinal.'

Third. Again, as there is variety in a feast, so there is *sufficiency, full sufficiency*. 'We beheld the only begotten Son of God, full of grace and truth,' John 1:14. And being full of grace, he is wise, and able to furnish this heavenly banquet with enough of all sorts of provisions fit for the soul to feed upon. There is abundance of grace, and excellency, and sufficiency in Christ. And it must needs be, because he is a Saviour of God's own sending. 'Labour not therefore for the meat that perisheth, but for the meat that the Son of God shall give you; for him hath God the Father sealed,' John 6:27; that is, sent forth for this purpose, to 'feed the church of God,' 1 Pet. 5:2. As there is an all-sufficiency in God, so in Christ, who by the sacrificing of himself was able to give satisfaction to divine justice. Therefore saith he, 'My flesh is meat indeed, and my blood is drink indeed,' John 6:55; that is, spiritually to the soul he is food indeed, and can satisfy God's justice. If we consider him as God alone, he is a 'consuming fire,' Heb. 12:29; or as a man alone, he can do nothing; but considered as God-man, he is meat indeed, and drink indeed. And now the soul is content with that which divine justice is contented withal. Though our conscience be large, yet God is larger and above our consciences. Therefore, as there is variety of excellency, so is there sufficiency and fulness in Christ. What he did, he did to the full. He is a Saviour, and he filleth up that name to the full. His pardon for sin is a full pardon; his merits for us are full merits; his satisfaction to divine justice a full satisfaction; his redemption of our souls and bodies a full redemption. Thus all he did was full.

Fourth. A feast is for company. It is *convivium.* There is converse at it. So Cicero prefers the name of *convivium* among the Latins before the Greek name συμπόσιον *symposion.*[1] And this feast is not for one. We are all invited to it. The excellency of Christ's feast consisteth in the communion of saints; for whosoever takes part of it, their spirits must agree one with another. Love is the best and chiefest dish in this feast. The more we partake of the sweetness of Christ, the more we love one another. Christ by his Spirit so works in the hearts of the children of men, that, bring a thousand together of a thousand several nations, and within a little while you shall have them all acquainted one with another. If they be good, there is agreement of the spirit and sympathy between them. There is a kindred in Christ. He is the true Isaac. The death of Christ and the blood of Christ is the ground of all union and joy and comfort whatsoever. The blood of Christ sprinkled upon the conscience will procure that peace of conscience that shall be a continual feast unto the soul. This feast must needs be wonderful comfortable, for we do not feast with those that are like ourselves, but we feast with God the Father, and the Holy Spirit, sent by Christ, procured by the death of Christ. The angels at this feast attend us; therefore, it must needs be joyful. No joy comparable to the joy of a feast. This is not every feast. This is a marriage feast, at which we are contracted to Christ.

[1] 'Cicero prefers the name of convivium.' The allusion is to Cicero's *De Senectute* (on Old Age), 13 *fin*, which may be here quoted: – 'For our fathers did well in calling the reclining of friends at feasts a *convivium*, because it implies a communion of life, which is a better designation than that of the Greeks, who call it sometimes a "drinking together" and sometimes an "eating together."'

Now, of all feasts, marriage feasts are most sumptuous. This is a marriage feast for the King's Son, for Christ himself; and therefore of necessity it must be full of all choice varieties, and of the sweetest of things, of the most excellentest of things, and of the quintessence of things. Here is all joy that belongeth to a feast. Here it is to be had with Christ. What acquaintance can be more glorious than that which is to be had between Jesus Christ and a Christian soul? when we have hope of better things to come, then we find the sweetness of this communion. No harmony in the world can be so sweet as the harmony maintained between Christ and the soul. When we have this, and are made one with God in Christ, our joy must needs then be unspeakable. When the contract is once made between the soul and Christ, there cannot but be abundant joy. When the soul is joined with Christ by faith, it cannot but solace itself in a perpetual jubilee and a perpetual feast in some degrees.

Fifth. Again, for a feast ye have the choicest garments, as at the marriage of the Lamb, 'white and fine linen,' Rev. 19:8, which is the righteousness of the saints. When God seeth these robes upon us and the Spirit of Christ in us, then there is a robe of righteousness imputed, and a garment of sanctity, whereby our souls are clothed. So this is a feast that must have wonderful glorious attire; and when this marriage shall be consummated, we are sure to have a garment of glory put upon us.

Sixth. This was signified in old time by the Jews.
1. In the feast of the passover (not to name all resemblances, but only one or two). *The lamb for the passover*, you know, was chosen out of the flock from amongst the

rest four days before the time appointed for that feast. So Christ is the true Paschal Lamb, chosen of God before the foundation of the world was laid, to be slain for us.

2. Again, *manna* was a type of Christ. It came from heaven to feed the hungry bodies of the Israelites in the wilderness. Even so came Christ, sent from God the Father, to be the eternal food and upholder of the souls and bodies of every one of us. Manna was white and sweet; so was Christ, white in righteousness and holiness, and also sweet to delight the soul. Manna fell upon the tents in the night; and Christ came when darkness was spread over all the world. God gave manna freely from heaven; so Christ was a free gift, and he freely gave himself to death, even to the cursed death of the cross, for us. All, both poor and rich, they gathered manna. Christ is a common food for king and subject. All take part of Christ. Neither Jew nor Gentile are exempted, but all may come and buy freely without money. Of this manna he that had least had enough. So here he that hath least of Christ, though he take him with a trembling hand, yet he shall have enough, for Christ is his. Whosoever hath the least grace, if it be true and sound, hath grace enough to bring him to eternal life. The Jews wondered at the manna, saying, What thing is this?[1] So it is one of Christ's names to be called 'Wonderful,' Isa. 9:6. Grace and favour from Christ is true spiritual manna to the soul. Manna fell in the wilderness: even so must we remain in the wilderness of this wretched world until we come to heaven. Christ is manna to us, and very sweet in the conveyance of his word

---

[1] 'The Jews wondered at the manna, saying, What thing is this?' 'Manna,' meaning 'What's this?' itself expresses and records their wonder.

and sacraments. When the Israelites came into the land of Canaan the manna ceased, not before. So when we come to heaven, the elect's purchased possession, we shall have another kind of manna for our souls. We shall not there feed on Christ, as in the sacrament; no, but we shall see him 'face to face, and know as we are known,' 1 Cor. 13:12. In the wilderness of this world it is fit God should convey this heavenly manna to the soul whatsoever way he pleaseth. Manna could not fall until the Israelites had spent all the provision they brought with them out of Egypt; and we cannot taste of that heavenly manna of our Father until our souls are drawn away from all worldly dependences and carnal delights. Then, indeed, manna will be sweet and precious.

What is this heavenly manna, what is Christ and his Father, what is the word and sacraments, to a depraved, vicious heart, stuffed full with earthly vanities? Alas! it loatheth all these. As none tasted of manna but those that came out of Egypt, so none shall taste of Christ but those that are not of the world, that are come out of Egypt, out of sin and darkness. Manna fell only about the tents of Israel, and in no other part of the world, but only there, that none might have the privilege to eat of it but God's peculiar, chosen ones. Christ falls upon the tents of the righteous, and none shall taste of this blessed, spiritual food but such as are the Israel of God, such as are of the church, such as feel the burden of sin and groan under it. Oh! the very taste of this heavenly manna is sweet to their souls, and to none but them. Thus ye see the feast that Christ maketh for us in mount Zion, and that this manna doth typify Christ with all his benefits.

3. Again, *the hard rock in the wilderness*, when it was strucken[1] with the rod of Moses, presently water gushed out in abundance, which preserved life to the Israelites; so Christ, the rock of our salvation, the strength of his church, the rock and fortress of all his saints, when his precious side was gored with the bloody lance upon the cross, the blood gushed out, and in such a manner and such abundance, that by the shedding thereof our souls are preserved alive. He is both manna and the rock of water. Manna had all in it, so had the rock; and all necessities are plentifully supplied by Christ. The church of God hath always had bread to satisfy spiritual hunger. It never wanted necessary comforts. It is said, Rev. 12:6, 'When the church fled into the wilderness, God fed her there,' alluding to the children of Israel fed by manna. The Jews did not want in the wilderness, nor the church of God never wanted comfort, though in the midst of the persecution and oppression of all her enemies. When Elijah was in the wilderness, he was fed, 1 Kings 17:4, 6. The church of God shall not only be fed in her body, but in her soul, for Christ hath hidden manna for his elect. This doth typify the exceeding joy of the church, the hidden manna, 'that neither eye hath seen, nor ear heard of, neither can it enter into the heart of man to conceive of those joys,' 1 Cor. 2:9, that the church of God shall have when the marriage shall be consummated. Joy in the Holy Ghost, and peace of conscience, they are hid from the world, and sometimes from God's people themselves, though they shall enjoy them hereafter.

4. *All the former feasts* in times past were but types of this. The feast of tabernacles, the feast of the passover,

[1] That is, 'struck.'

the spiritual manna, and all other holy feasts, were but to signify and to shew forth this feast by Christ. But there is this difference between the type and the thing signified. By the type, the passover lamb was quite eaten up; but this passover, Christ, that was slain for sin, can never be eaten up. We feed upon him with our souls. He cannot be consumed as the passover lamb, nor as manna, which was gone when the sun arose. Yea, that manna that was laid up for a remembrance before the ark, became nothing, but Christ is in heaven for evermore for the soul to feed upon. Though these were resemblances, yet these failed, as it is fit resemblances should fail, that is, come short of the body of the thing itself. Thus you see the spiritual comforts of a Christian may well and fitly be compared to a feast.

Thus you see God provideth a feast, and inviteth all. *In the sacrament you have a feast*, a feast of varieties, not only bread, but wine – to shew the variety and fulness of comfort in Christ. He intendeth full comfort. As for our adversaries the papists, they have dry feasts. They give the people the bread, but the wine they keep for themselves. But God in Christ intendeth us full comfort. Whatsoever Christ did, it was full. His merits are complete, and his joy was full. He is fulness itself; and, therefore, whatsoever comes from him must needs be, as he himself is, both full and sweet. He intendeth us full consolation.

Use 1. Therefore, we ought to be prepared to partake of this feast, in such a manner as that we may have full joy, and full comfort; for there is in Christ enough to satisfy all the hungry souls in the world, he himself being present at this heavenly banquet. 'All fulness dwells in him,' Col.

1:19, from which 'we have all received, and grace for grace.'
Therefore,

Let us labour to have large hearts: for as our faith groweth
more and more, so we shall carry more comfort and more
strength from this holy feast. As the poor widow, if her
vessels had not failed, the oil had not ceased; if there had
been more vessels, there had been more oil, 2 Kings 4:6.
Our souls are as these vessels. Let us therefore labour, and
make it our great business to have large souls, souls capable
to drink in this spiritual oil of gladness; for as much faith
as we bring to Christ, so much comfort we shall carry from
him. The favours of God in Christ being infinite, the more
we fetch from him, the more glory we give unto him. But
if they were finite, we should offend his bounty, he might
soon be drawn dry, and so send us away with an uncom-
fortable answer, that he was not able to relieve us. But
Christ is infinite, and the more we have from him, the more
we may have. 'To him that hath shall be given,' Matt. 13:12.
The oftener we go to Christ, the more honour and glory we
bring unto him. This is a banquet to the full.

We are now come to the banquet, and Christ is the
founder of it; nay, he is the feast itself. He is the author of it,
and he it is that we feed upon.

Use 2. Let us labour not to be straight[1] receivers of the
sacrament, but suck in abundance from Christ with a great
deal of delight, that we may come together not for the worse
but the better, considering what a great deal of strength and
grace is required as very necessary for the maintaining of
spiritual life.

[1] Qu. 'strait.'

Sermon 2

In this mountain shall the Lord of hosts make unto all people a feast of fat things, a feast of wines on the lees; of fat things full of marrow, of wine on the lees well refined.
— Isaiah 25:6

I HAVE shewed that Christ and his benefits are compared to a feast, and in what respects they are fitly resembled by a feast, and have pressed that we should prepare for it, first by getting large hearts.

Use. 2 (cont'd). Now, in the *second* place, that we may have comfort at this feast, *we must labour for spiritual appetite*; for to what end and purpose is that man at a feast that hath no stomach? I shall therefore shew what means we are to use to get eager stomachs and holy appetites after this feast.

(1.) *The appetite is raised with sour things*, as anguish of spirit and mournfulness of heart for sin. If we will ever relish Christ aright, we must labour to have a quick apprehension of our sins. We must do as the Jews did at the passover. They ate it with sour herbs, that they might thereby have the sharper stomachs. So must we. We must cast our eyes into our own hearts, and consider what vile wretches we are, how full of sin and vanity; and this will be as sour herbs to the Paschal Lamb. We must join the sweet benefits and privileges that we have in Christ with the consideration of our own wretched and miserable condition, and then this heavenly ordinance cannot but be sweet and comfortable to our souls. I beseech you, enter into your own souls, and consider seriously under what guilt you lie, and this will whet your appetite. 'A full stomach despiseth the honeycomb,' Prov. 27:7; but in this appetite there is sense of emptiness, and from that sense of emptiness pain, and from pain an earnest desire of satisfaction. Thus it is in spiritual things. We want Christ, and all the spiritual comforts that flow from him. There is an emptiness in us, and we see a need every day to feed upon the mercies of God in Christ. There is an emptiness in our souls, and there must be a sense of that emptiness, and pain from that sense, which must stir up a strong endeavour to follow after that that we do desire. Then Christ indeed is sweet, when we find our souls hungering and thirsting after him.

(2.) Again, if so be we would have that appetite of spirit that is fit for this feast, *we must purge our souls from the corruptions of flesh and spirit*, 'perfecting holiness in the fear of God,' 2 Cor. 7:1. We must cleanse our souls from those lusts and passions that daily cleave unto them. All crudities must be taken away, that the edge of the stomach may not be flatted:[1] for while these earthly carnal corruptions lie upon the soul, we can expect no spiritual appetite to heavenly things. Let us therefore examine ourselves, what filth lies upon our souls, and what corrupt inclinations are there, that so they may be purged, and our desires be carried fully after Christ in the sacrament.

---

[1] That is 'flattened,' = appetite destroyed. – G.

(3.) Another means to get appetite is *to consider thoroughly what is required of a Christian, well to maintain the trade of Christianity*. It is another manner of thing than we take it for, to entertain communion with God, to perform holy duties in an holy manner, to bear the yoke as a Christian should do. Here is a great deal of strength required; and because corruptions will mix themselves amongst our best performances, there must be a great deal of mercy from God to pardon them. And whence is all this but by the death of our blessed Saviour Jesus Christ? For his sake, God hath a forbearing eye. Now, if we consider what a degree of spiritual strength and vigour we should have to go through with these duties, this would sharpen our stomachs and spiritual appetites, to furnish ourselves with grace from Christ to go through with these holy services. There must be an exercising of all the duties of Christianity, which is an estate that must be maintained with a great deal of charge and labour. A man can do no service acceptable to God but by grace; and grace must feed the soul with fruitful knowledge in the power of faith. And when the soul feeleth a necessity of grace, oh! then, beloved, it hungers and earnestly thirsteth after the love of God in Christ. We need to every trade a great deal of knowledge. Then surely the calling of Christianity needeth a great deal. A Christian must expect much both in prosperity and adversity, as the apostle saith, 'I have learned to want and to abound, to be in honour and to be in disgrace, and I can do all things through Christ that strengthens me,' Phil. 4:12. Now, because there is so much goings so, out for the maintenance of Christianity, we must also bring in much grace, and faith, and love, and holiness, or else we shall never be able to uphold this condition. Where there is an exercise of Christianity, there will be an appetite to heaven; that is our best calling. For when that we have done all that we can, that, that we must have comfort from, is Christianity. Therefore, labour with all labour to be holy and able Christians. All other callings are but for this present life; but that that is for eternity is this calling of Christianity. And this is only to fit us here in this world for an everlasting condition of glory in the world to come.

(4.) Again, if we would have a desire and appetite to heavenly things, *we must labour to get acquaintance, and constantly converse with those that are good.* The old proverb is, 'Company will make a man fall to,' especially the company of those that are better than ourselves. For very emulation, men will be doing as others do. When men live amongst those whose hearts are framed this way, they must be equal. Conversation with those that have good relish of spiritual things, and shew forth grace in their lives, setteth an appetite upon our desires, to desire the same things that they do. Thus St Paul writeth to the Gentiles to stir up the emulation of the Jews. Therefore receive this likewise for the procuring of a spiritual appetite. To go on.

(5.) The next thing that may stir up our desires to get an appetite to the best things, is seriously to consider, *that we cannot tell how long we have to live, or may enjoy the benefit of the means of grace.* Those that sit at table and discourse away the greatest part of dinner time in talk, had need at last to fall to so much the faster, by how much the more negligent they had been before in eating. We cannot tell how long we may enjoy this spiritual feast that God makes for us. Therefore, be stirred up to get spiritual appetites; for we

know not how long God will spread a table for us. We know
not how long we shall enjoy our lives; and if we be surprised
on the sudden, we may suffer a spiritual famine, a famine
of the soul, if we have nothing to comfort us beforehand;
and of all famines, a spiritual famine is most grievous, most
fearful. Therefore do as Joseph did, and be wise. He in the
seven years of plenty gathered for seven years of famine that
was to come upon the land of Egypt, Gen. 41:36, *seq*. Alas! if
we have nothing laid up beforehand, what will be our end?
We shall lie open to God's wrath and anger. Nothing can
support our souls in the evil time. Wherefore, as you desire
at that day to have comfort of those things ye shall stand
most in need of, labour to get a good appetite. For to perish
and starve at a feast is a shame; to famish in the liberty of
the gospel and plenty of spiritual meat, is shameful and
dishonourable. Thus you see, beloved, not to be large in the
point, how you may procure such an appetite as is fit for
such an holy feast. First, by getting a sense of sin; secondly,
by seeing a necessity of Christ; thirdly, by purging out those
lusts that lie upon the soul; fourthly, by conversing with
those that are spiritually minded; and lastly, by considering
the time to come.

Use 3. It is not enough to have a stomach, but we must
have *a spiritual disposition of soul to heavenly things, as
we have to outward things*. Labour to have a taste of good
things, and a distinguishing taste of heavenly things from
other things. God is the God of nature, and hath furnished
us with five senses; and as he hath given us sense to apprehend, so he hath furnished the creature with varieties of
excellences, suitable to all our several senses. He will not

have objects in the creature without sense, nor sense in man without objects. He hath furnished man with senses, and variety of senses, and given fit and proportionable objects for those senses. The soul also hath her sense. Wheresoever there is life, there is sense. God having given spiritual life to the soul, he doth maintain that life with spiritual food. As in a feast there is sight, and the eye is not only fed there with rich furniture, but with variety of dainties; the ear likewise and the smell is satisfied, the one with music, the other with sweet savours. So in this feast there is to delight both the ear and the smell of the soul, the one with hearing the gracious promises of Jesus Christ, and the other in receiving the sweet savour of that sacrifice that was offered up once for all. Nothing so sweet to the soul as the blessings of Christ. He is sweet in the word, as the vessel that conveyeth him into our souls. Thus you see in this feast all the senses, the sight, the smell, the taste, and hearing, all are satisfied, and a great care had, in the provision for the feast, that our outward man may be pleased. And shall the Lord of hosts make a feast, and not content the whole man? He is for our sight, if we have spiritual eyes to see; the ear, if we have ears to hear. All the senses are exercised here. What is the reason why carnal men cannot relish a pardon for sin, and justification, and sanctification, and holiness, nor go boldly to God? It may be they have good, sweet notions of these, but they have no spiritual taste or relish of them, and all because they want spiritual life. None but a Christian can have spiritual taste answerable to a spiritual life. Taste is a kind of feeling, one of the most necessary senses; and a Christian can not be without relish and feeling. Yea, it is the very being of a Christian to have a taste of spiritual things.

Of all other senses, there is a stronger application in taste. The other senses fetch their objects afar off; but as for taste, there is a near application in it, and therefore most necessary. Every life is maintained by taste. 'Taste and see how good the Lord is,' Psa. 34:8.

Now, taste doth two things; it doth relish that that is good, and disrelish the contrary. There must be a spiritual taste to discern of differences. There can be no spiritual taste but it must know what is good and profitable for the soul, and what is not. Because God will not have our tastes to be wronged, ye see what course he takes. First, the eye seeth what things we taste on, and if the eye be displeased, so also is the smell. Thus God layeth before us spiritual things, knowledge of good and bad, and giveth us many caveats, and all because he would not have us to taste things hurtful for the soul, nor poison instead of meat. Now, when we have tasted that which is good, let us take heed it be not a taste only, lest we fall into the sin against the Holy Ghost.

Use 4. Again, beside taste, *there must be a digesting of what we taste, and that thoroughly, in our understandings.* When we apprehend a thing to be true and good, it must be digested thoroughly into the affections. Love to the best things must be above all other love whatsoever; yet this must be digested. Men oftentimes have sweet notions, but, alas! they are but notions; they do not digest them into their affections. It is the last digestion that nourisheth; and when any spiritual truths are understood thoroughly, then comes in spiritual strength; and hereupon the soul comes and sucks in that virtue which is for the nourishment of it. Thus it is in the soul; upon digestion there is nourishment.

Again, there must be a faculty to retain what we have received, that it may be digested. Ye have many that love to hear, but they do not digest. If there be nothing in the soul, nothing can be extracted; and therefore we must learn to retain necessary truths, that so upon occasion they may come from the memory into the heart. Though, indeed, they are not in their proper place when they are in the memory only, yet notwithstanding, if they are there, they may with ease be brought down into the soul.

Use 5. Then we must labour to walk in the strength of spiritual things. For what is the use of this feast but to cherish both soul and spirit? The use of spiritual things which we have through Christ is to cherish and enliven. It conveyeth strength to us, that we may walk in the strength of Christ, as Elijah did forty days in the strength of his food, 1 Kings 19:8. And consider, though in our consciences and conditions we have variety of changes, yet in Christ we have several comforts suitable to all our several conditions. If so be our sins trouble us, we should watch over ourselves, that we be not over much cast down, but feed upon spiritual things in consideration of pardon for sin in the blood of Christ. This is the grand issue of all that Christ hath traced out in the forgiveness of sins. He is not, he cannot be divided. Where he pardons sins, he sanctifieth; where he sanctifieth, he writes his law in their hearts. So that there is a chain of spiritual favours. Where the first link is, all the rest follow. Where forgiveness of sin is, there is the Spirit, and that Spirit sanctifieth, and comforts, and is an earnest of everlasting life. Therefore, feed especially upon the favours of God, and get forgiveness of sins, and then all the rest of the chain of grace and spiritual life will follow.

Sometimes we stand in need of present grace and comfort, and we are undone if comforts and grace are not at hand, never considering the promises that are to come; as that promise of Christ, 'I will be with thee to the end of the world, fear not,' Matt. 28:20. No temptation shall befall us, but we shall have an issue out of it, and it shall work together for the good of all those that fear God. This is *aqua vitae*[1] to the soul of man. Therefore the gracious promises of Christ and his Holy Spirit we should ever remember to get into our souls; for when all other comforts fail, then cometh in the comforts of the Spirit, who will be with us and uphold us in all extremities. If we had nothing in this world to comfort our spirits, yet let us rejoice in hope of glory to come. 'Our life is hid with Christ,' Col. 3:3. We have 'the hidden manna,' Rev. 2:17. 'In him we rejoice in hope of glory,' Rom. 5:2. And the way to maintain a Christian, holy life, is to make use of all the privileges of Christianity, and of those promises that convey these privileges to our souls.

Now that we may the better do this, observe continually what it is that hinders us, that we cannot feed upon spiritual things as we should do. Whatsoever it is, we must labour constantly to remove it.

Now, what must follow after this feast? (1.) Why! *spiritual cheerfulness!* If we find this in our duties of Christianity, it is a sign we have fed upon spiritual things. The nature of a spiritual feast is to empty the soul of sin, and to fill it full of gracious thoughts and actions. Instead thereof it moderates all things. It makes us use the world as if we used it not.

[1] Latin: 'water of life.'

When we can do this, we may certainly know that our souls have tasted of abundance of benefit by this feast.

A man that hath no spiritual joy is drowned for the most part in the contentments of the world, drowned in riches and honours; and these are like to strong waters immoderately taken, instead of cheering the spirits, [they] exhaust and kill them. He that hath the joy of heaven here by faith, is mortified to all other base delights, 'he only mindeth the things above, where Christ is,' Col. 3:1. And therefore the exhortation, or rather command, 'Seek the things that are above,' hath this promise in fit method annexed to it, 'and then all other things shall be cast in upon you,' Matt. 6:33. Riches and honours in the world; and if not them, yet so much as is necessary, and mortification of our sins, and the lusts of the flesh.

Again, if we have fed upon spiritual things for our souls, (2.) *we shall be thankful.* That man that hath tasted how good and gracious the Lord hath been to him in this world, and how full of joy and comfort he will be to him in another world, in consideration of this, his soul cannot choose but be thankful to God.

Here we see how to make this spiritual food fit for our souls, that Christ provideth for us. And if there be such joy as we have said there is in spiritual things, what use should we make further of them, but labour from hence (3.) *to justify the ways of godliness against our own false and carnal hearts, and against the slanderous imputations of the world.* When our hearts are ready to be false to us, and hanker after the contentments of the world, and are ready to say the best contentments that they can enjoy is in the things below; let us answer our base and false disputing hearts, that the ways of wisdom, the ways that God directs us to, they only are the ways of pleasure. And religion is that that makes the hearts of the children of men joyful; and 'a good conscience only makes a continual feast,' Prov. 15:15, so long as man liveth. But especially at the hour of death, when all the comforts of the world cease, then conscience standeth our friend.

Objection. But the world's objection is, that of all kind of men in the world, those that profess religion are the most melancholy.

Answer. But if it be so, it is because they are not religious enough. Their sins are continually before their eyes. They have pardon for sin, and freedom from the guilt of sin, but know it not. They have good things, and do not know them. And so in regard of spiritual comforts, God's people may have spiritual joy, and inward consolation, and yet not know of it. There may be such a time when they may be sad and droop, and that is when they apprehend God doth not look pleasantly upon them. But the true character of a Christian is to be cheerful, and none else can be truly cheerful and joyous. Joy is usurped by others. There is no comfort in them that can be said to be real. All the joy of a man that is a carnal man is but as it were the joy of a traitor. He may come to the sacraments, and feast with the rest of God's people, but what mirth or joy can he have so long as the Master of the feast frowns upon him? Where Christ is not, there God is not reconciled. No joy like that joy of him that is assured of the love of God in Christ. A man may sometime through ignorance want that joy that belongeth to him. 'Rejoice, ye righteous, and be glad,' Psa. 33:1. It belongeth to those that are in Christ and to the righteous to rejoice, for joy is all their portion. They only can justify the ways of God against all reproaches whatsoever. But the eyes of carnal men are so held in blindness, that they can see no joy, no comfort in this course. As it is said of Augustine before his conversion, he was afraid to turn Christian indeed, lest he should want[1] all those joys and pleasures that the world did then afford him; but after he was converted, then he could cry, 'Lord, I have stayed too long from thee,' and too long delayed from coming in to taste of the sweetness of Jesus Christ.[2]

Take a Christian at the worst, and he is better than another man, take him at the best. The worst condition of God's children far surpasseth the very best condition of graceless persons. The issue of things shall turn to his good that is a member of Christ, a child of God, an heir of heaven. The evil of evils is taken away from him. Take him at the worst, he is an heir of heaven; but take the wicked at the best, he is not a child of God, he is a stranger to God, he is as a branch cut off, and as miserable a wretch as ever Belshazzar in the midst of his cups, trembling and quaking with fear and astonishment, when he saw the writing on the wall, Dan. 5:24, *seq*. When a man apprehends the wrath of God hanging over his head, though he were in the greatest feast in the world, and amongst those that make mirth and jollity, yet seeing vengeance ready to seize upon him, it cannot but damp all his joy and all his carnal pleasures; and therefore only a Christian hath a true title to this feast.

---

[1] That is, 'be in want of' or 'lack.'

[2] *Confessions*, Book X. [xxvii]. 88. 'Too late loved I thee, O thou beauty of ancient days, yet ever new! too late I loved thee.' – G.

I beseech you, let us labour earnestly to have our part and portion in the things above. But what shall they do, that as yet apprehend no interest in Jesus Christ? Why! let them not be discouraged, for all are compelled to come into this feast, both blind and lame. The servants are sent to bring them in. The most wretched people of all, God doth invite them. All are called to come in to this feast that are sensible of their sins; and that, God requires at our hands, or else we can have no appetite to taste of this feast. God saith, 'Come all,' Isa. 55:1. Aye, but, saith the poor, sinful soul, I have no grace at all! Why! but yet come, 'buy without money'; the feast is free. 'God's thoughts are not as thy thoughts are'; 'but as heaven is high above the earth, even so are his thoughts above thy thoughts,' Isa. 55:8, 9. Poor wretch! thou thinkest thou hast led a wicked life, and so thou hast! Aye, but now come in, God hath invited thee, and he will not always be inviting thee. Therefore come in, and study the excellencies of Christ. When such persons as these see they need mercy, and grace, and reconciliation, and must either have it or else be damned forever, now they are earnest to study the favour and love of God in Christ; now they bestir themselves to get peace of conscience and joy in the Holy Ghost; now they see salvation to be founded only on Christ, and all other excellencies belonging to Christianity; and therefore he goeth constantly provided with grace and holiness, so in this life that he may not lose his part in glory in the life to come. Think of this and pray for it, as they in the gospel. 'Lord, evermore give me of that bread,' John 6:34. Here is hope that thou mayest be saved, because thou art invited to come in. To what end is the ministry of the gospel, but to entreat thee to be reconciled? Oh! let this work upon our souls when we hear of the excellencies of these things! And together with them, consider of the necessity that is cast upon us to obtain them, and that we must have them or else be damned eternally. We must do as the lepers did, who said one to another, 'Why sit we here till we die? If we say, We will enter into the city, why, the famine is in the city, and we shall die there: and if we sit still here, we shall also die.' Now, what course took they? 'They said one to another, Let us enter into the camp of the Syrians, there is meat to feed us,' 2 Kings 7:3, 4. So saith the soul, If I go into the city of the world, there I shall be starved; if I sit still, I shall also perish. What shall I now do? I will venture upon Jesus Christ; he hath food that endures to eternal life, and if I perish there, I perish. If I have not Christ I must die, the wrath of God hangeth over my head, and I cannot escape. Alas! poor soul, now thou seest thy wretchedness, cast thyself upon him, and come in. If thou venturest, thou canst but die! Adventure therefore, put thyself upon God's mercy, for he is gracious and full of compassion.

Those that have given up themselves to Christ, let them study to honour God and Christ, by taking those comforts that are allotted to them. When any man inviteth us to a feast, he knoweth if we respect him we will fall to. God hath bestowed his Son upon us, and will he not with him give us all things? Let us not therefore dishonour the bounty of our good God, but come in, and labour to have our hearts more and more enlarged with the consideration of the excellency of these eternal comforts. The fulness of Christ is able to satisfy the soul, though it were a thousand times larger than it is. If it were possible that we could get the capacity of angels, it could not be sufficient to shew forth the fulness of pleasures that are provided for a Christian. Let us therefore labour with all labour to open our hearts to entertain these joys, for we cannot honour God more than of his bounty to receive thankfully what he freely offers. To taste plentifully in the covenant of grace, of these riches, and joy, and hope of things to come, glorious above all that we are able to think of; I say, this is the way to honour God under the gospel of hope. Of things that are infinite, the more we take, the more we may take, and the more we honour him that giveth. Let us therefore enter deeply into our special sins, there is no fear of despair. Think of all thy wants, and of all thy sins; let them be never so many, yet there is more to be had in Christ than there can be wanting in thee. The soul that thinks itself full of wants is the richest soul, and that that apprehendeth no want at all, no need of grace or Christ, is always sent empty away. Grieve therefore for thy sins, and then joy that thou hast grieved, and go to God for the supply of all thy wants. The seeds of joy and of comfort are sown in tears and grief in this world; but yet we know we shall reap in joy in the world to come.

Remember this, we have we know not what to go through withal in this valley of tears. That speech of Barzillai was good and excellent, who being by David himself invited to the court, answered, 'I am now grown old, I am not fit for the court, for my senses are decayed and gone,' 2 Sam. 19:32, *seq.* Even so the time will come when our sense of relishing earthly pleasures will utterly be lost. We are sure to go to our graves, and we know not what particular trouble we may meet with in this world and go through, if we live to a full age. Alas! what are all comforts here to the comforts of eternity? When our days are spent on earth, then comes in the eternity of pleasure or everlasting sorrow. Oh then if, when we shall leave all behind us, we have the joy of the Holy Ghost in our hearts, it will advance us above all the suggestions of sin or Satan, and bring us cheerfully above to the tribunal seat of Christ. Labour therefore to have a spiritual relish of soul, to grow in grace and comforts of the Holy Ghost; for the time will come when we shall wish that we had had more than we have. Every one will repent of looseness and slackness in the ways of holiness. Therefore let us labour earnestly to be good husbands for our souls for the time to come.

Sermon 3

*In this mountain shall the Lord of hosts make unto all
people a feast, etc. And he will destroy in this mountain
the face of the covering cast over all people, and the veil
that is spread over all nations.*

– Isaiah 25:6, 7

I HAVE heretofore spoken of the feast that God makes to
his church, specially in the latter times, which was specially
performed at the first coming of Christ, when the Gentiles
came in; but the consummation and perfection of all will
be at the day of judgment. Then God will spread a table for
his to all eternity.

We have spoken heretofore at large of the resemblance
of spiritual good things, by this comparison of a feast. God
sets out spiritual things by outward, because we cannot
otherwise conceive of them; the best things in grace, by the
best and sweetest things in nature. And thus God enters
into our souls by our senses, as we see in the sacrament.

But we have spoken at large of this. Our care must be to
have a special taste, a spiritual appetite to relish this feast
that God provides. Naturally we are distasteful. We relish
not spiritual and heavenly things; we savour not the things
of God. And the Spirit of God must alter our savour and
taste, as he doth. Wheresoever there is spiritual life, there is
spiritual relish of heavenly truths.

Now let me add this further, *that though it be made by God, yet we must bring something to this feast.* Christ feasteth with us, as ye have, Rev. 3:20. He sups with us, not that we have grace from ourselves, or can bring anything; he bringeth his own provision with him when he suppeth with us; but yet by the covenant of grace whereby he enters into terms of friendship with us, we must sup with him, we must have grace to entertain him, though it is at his own cost; yet we must have something. He doth not require us to pay our debts, but he giveth us wherewith. Secretly he bids us come, but giveth a secret messenger to draw us; he sends his Spirit certainly. Certainly he will have us bring something when we come to feast, but it is of his own giving. And that we are to bring is humble and empty souls, wherein we are to delight ourselves in sense of our unworthiness; and the spirit of faith to believe his promises. That pleaseth him, when we can honour him with a spirit of faith, and then a spirit of love, and new obedience springing from a spirit of faith and love. These be the things Christ requires we should have. Our souls must be thus furnished that Christ may delight to dwell with us; and therefore it is a good importuning of God, 'Lord, I desire thou shouldst dwell in me, and prepare my soul as a fit temple'; 'vouchsafe me the graces thou delightest in, and delightest to dwell in.' So we may beg of God his Holy Spirit to furnish our souls, so as he may dwell and delight in us.

But we have spoken largely of the former verse. I will now speak of the next that followeth.

'*And I will destroy in this mountain the face of covering cast over all people, and the veil spread over all nations, to swallow up death in victory; the Lord will wipe away tears from all faces; and the rebukes of his people shall be taken from the earth, for the Lord hath spoken it.'*

These depend one upon another, being the several services of the feast. He promiseth a feast in the sixth verse. And what be the several services? He will destroy in this mountain, this church, the face of covering cast over all people, etc. He will take away the veil of ignorance and unbelief, that they may have special sight of heavenly things, without which they cannot relish heavenly things; they can take no joy at this feast.

And then, because there can be no feast, where there is the greatest enemy in force and power, he swallows up death in victory. Death keeps us in fear all our lifetime. That that swalloweth up all kings and monarchs, the terror of the world, death, shall be and is swallowed up by our head, Christ, and shall be swallowed up by us in victory. In the meantime we are subject to many sorrows which cause tears; for tears are but drops that issue from that cloud of sorrow; and sorrow we have always in this world, either from sins or miseries, or sympathy in tears of that kind. Well, the time will come that tears shall be wiped away, and the cause of tears; all sorrow for our own sins, for our own misery, and for sympathizing with the times wherein we live. Our time shall be hereafter at the day of resurrection, when all tears shall be wiped from our eyes. God will perform that office of a mother to wipe the children's eyes, or of a nurse to take away all cause of grief whatsoever, else it cannot be a perfect feast.

Aye, but there are reproaches cast upon religion and religious persons! It goeth under a veil of reproach, and the best things are not seen in their own colours; nor the worst things; they go under vizards here.

But the time will come that the rebukes of his people shall be taken away. The good things, as they are best, so shall they be known to be so; and sin, and base courses, as they are bad, and as they are from hell, so they shall be known to be. Everything shall appear in its own colours; things shall not go masked any longer. And what is the seal of all this? The seal of it is, 'The mouth of the Lord hath spoken it.' Truth itself hath spoken it, and therefore it must needs be. Jehovah, that can give a being to all things, he hath said it.

We have heard why the church is called a mountain. He will destroy, or swallow up,[1] as the word may signify, the face of covering, or the covering of the face; the veil which is the covering of the face, and particularly expressed in that term always; the veil that is spread over all nations.

God will take away the spiritual veil that covers the souls of his people, that is between them and divine truths. It hath allusion to that of Exod. 34:34, 35, about Moses when he came from the mount. He had a veil, for the people could not behold him. He had a glory put upon his face, that they could not look upon him with a direct eye, and therefore he was fain to put a veil upon his face, to shew that the Jews could not see, as Paul interprets it, 2 Cor. 3:15, 'To this day,' saith he, 'when Moses is read, there is a veil put upon their hearts.' They could not see that 'the law was a schoolmaster to bring to Christ,' Gal. 3:24, the ceremonial law and the moral law. God had a blessed end, by the curse

[1] 'Swallow.' – Dr J. A. Alexander in his *Commentary* adopts the rendering of Sibbes here.

of it, to bring them to Christ. They rested in the veil, their sight was terminated in the veil, they could not see through to the end and scope of it. Nevertheless, when they shall turn to the Lord, the veil shall be taken away.

1. From the words, consider first of all, *that naturally there is a veil of ignorance upon the soul.*

2. *Secondly, God doth take away this veil*; and God by his Spirit only can do it.

3. *Thirdly, that this is only in his church.* And where this veil of ignorance is taken off, there is feasting with God and spiritual joy, and delight in the best order; and where it is not taken off there is none of it.

First of all, by nature, *there is a veil of covering over all men's spirits.* To understand this better, let us unfold the terms of veil a little. There is a veil either upon the things themselves that are to be seen, or upon the soul which should behold them.

(1.) The veil *of things themselves* is when they be hidden altogether, or in part; when we know part, and are ignorant of part. And this veil upon the things ariseth from the weak apprehension of them; when they are not represented in clear expressions, but in obscurity of words or types; when we see them only in types or obscure phrases, which hideth sometime the sight of the thing itself. The manner of speech sometimes casteth a veil on things; for our Saviour Christ spake in parables, which were like the cloud, dark on the one side, light on the other, dark towards the Egyptians, light towards the Israelites. So some expressions of Scripture have a light side, that only the godly see, and a dark side, that other men, good wits, as natural men, see not.

(2.) Again, there is a veil *upon the soul and upon the sight.* If the things be veiled, or the sight veiled, there is no sight. Now the soul is veiled when we be ignorant and unbelieving; when we are ignorant of what is spoken and revealed, or when we know the terms of it, and yet believe it not.

(3.) Now, this veil of ignorance and unbelief continueth in all unregenerate men *until grace takes away the veil.* Besides, before a thing can be seen, the object must not only be made clear, and the eyesight too, but there must be *lumen deferens,* a light to carry the object to the eye. If that be not, we cannot see. As the Egyptians, in the three days of darkness, had their eyes, but there wanted light to represent the object, and therefore they could not go near one to another. It is the light, and not sight. If there be sight and no light to carry and convey the object, we cannot say there is sight.

That which answereth to this veil is the veil of Scripture, whereby heavenly things are set out by a mystery. A mystery is, when something is openly shewed and something hidden.

When something is concealed, as in the sacrament, they be mysteries. We see the bread, we see the wine, but under the bread and wine other things are intended, the breaking of the body of Christ, and the shedding of his blood, and in that the love and mercy of God in Christ, in giving him to death for us, and Christ's love to give himself to satisfy divine justice. These be the things intended, which only the soul sees and apprehendeth. And so all things in the church, indeed, are mysteries, the incarnation of Christ, the union of both natures, that Christ should save the world by such a way as he did, that he should bring us to glory by shame, to life by death, to blessing and happiness by being a curse for us. It is a mystery to bring contrary out of contrary: that so glorious a person as God should be covered with our weak and sinful nature. It was a mystery, the Jews stumbled at it. Light came, and the darkness could not comprehend the light. And, as Christ was a mystery himself, so the church is a mystery. That God should so much delight in a company of poor men, the off-scouring of the world, to make them temples of his Holy Spirit, and heirs of heaven, men that were under the scorn of the world, this is a mystery. So all is mystical, the head, the members, the body, the church, and every particular point of religion. There is a mystery in repentance. No man knoweth what sorrow for sin is but the true gracious person. No man knows what it is to believe but he that hath an heart to believe. No man knoweth what peace of conscience and joy of the Holy Ghost is but those that feel it. So that is a mystery. And therefore 'great is the mystery of godliness,' saith the apostle, 1 Tim. 3:16. Not only in the points themselves, but even the practice of religion is a mystery too. Repentance and faith, and new obedience and love, and the comforts of religion, are all mysteries. There is a veil upon them in all these points, that a carnal man cannot see them.

You see, then, in what sense there is a veil of the things, and in what sense there is a veil on men's hearts; that is, either the things themselves are hid, or if the things be open, they want sight and light of knowledge, and they want faith to believe. Beloved, we live in times that the object is clear to us, the things themselves are made clear; as who knoweth not what Christ is, and the notion of the incarnation, and of the union with him. We know them notionally. They be opened and revealed to us very clearly, all the articles of faith, and mysteries of religion, so that there is no obscurity in the object. The things are clear, specially in these places of knowledge. But yet, notwithstanding, there is a veil upon the soul. The soul of every man that is not graciously wrought upon by the Spirit of God hath a veil of ignorance and unbelief.

First of all, *of ignorance*. There is a veil of ignorance in many, and in all men naturally a veil of ignorance of spiritual things. For, unless they be revealed, they can never be known to angels themselves. The angels themselves know not the gospel till it be opened, and therefore they be students in it continually, and the best men in the world know nothing in the gospel further than it is revealed. But there is a veil of ignorance upon them that know these things notionally, because they do not know them as they should know them; they do not know them *in propria specie*,[1] spiritual and heavenly things as spiritual and heavenly things. They do not know spiritual things as spiritual things, they have a human knowledge of spiritual things. Those that want grace, they know the grammar of the Scripture and divinity, and they know how to discourse as schoolmen do, from one thing to another, and to argue. They know the logic and rhetoric of the Scripture, but they stick in the stile. There is something they are ignorant of; that is, they have not an eye of knowledge, as we call it. They do not see the things themselves, but only they see things by another body's spirit, and they have no light of their own. And so no man knoweth naturally but the children of God what original sin is, what corruption of nature is, nor knows sin in its own odious colours,

[1] Latin: 'in their proper form.'

to be filthy, and to be dangerous as it is. To draw the curse and vengeance of God upon it, this is not known, but by the Spirit revealing the odiousness of sin, that the soul may apprehend it, as Christ did when he suffered for it, and as God doth. A gracious man seeth it as God seeth it, because by the Spirit of God he seeth the filthiness and odiousness of it, and the danger it draweth after it.

Second. And so in any points of religion naturally, *a man sees not them spiritually, as they are, and as God sees them, but he seeth them by a human light.* He seeth heavenly things by a human light, notionally, and merely to discourse of them. He seeth not intritively[1] into the things themselves. He seeth them *sub aliena specie*, under another representation than their own. Only a godly man seeth spiritual things as the Spirit of God, and seeth them as they are, knows sin as it is, knoweth grace to be as it is, and knoweth faith. What it is to believe, what it is to have peace of conscience, and the pardon of sins. He knoweth these things in some sense intritively, though not so as he shall do when he shall see these things in heaven, when he shall see face to face. There is a great difference in it. He sees them intritively in respect of the knowledge of other men, though he sees but in a glass in regard of the knowledge he shall have in heaven. As St Paul saith, 'For we see but as in a glass.' But he that sees in a glass seeth more life than he that sees the dead picture of a man. So, though we see but in a glass heavenly things, yet we see them better than those that see them in a dead notion. Though it be nothing to the knowledge we shall have in heaven, yet it is incomparable above the knowledge of any carnal natural man upon the earth.

[1] Qu. 'intuitively,' or 'interiorly'?; or, 'introitively'?

Third. Again, naturally men have veils of ignorance *upon the most divine things*. Of spiritual things, such as is union, and as is the communion between Christ and us, and the mystery of regeneration in the new creature, such as is the joy in the Holy Ghost, the inward peace of conscience. I will not name the particulars to insist on them, but give you only an instance. Though they know the notion of these things, yet they are altogether ignorant of them. Their knowledge is a mere outward light. It is a light radicated[1] in the soul. It is not as the light of the moon, which receiveth light from the sun, but it is a light radicated and incorporated into the soul, as the light of the sun is, by the Spirit. It is in the soul. It is not only upon the soul, but in the soul. The heart sees and feeleth, and knoweth divine truths. There is a power and virtue in the sight and knowledge of a gracious man. There is none in the knowledge of a carnal man. The light of a candle hath a light in it, but no virtue at all goeth with it; but the light of the sun, and the light of the stars, they have a special virtue, they have heat with them, and they have an influence in a special kind on inferior bodies working together with the light. So it is with heavenly apprehension and knowledge. It actually conveyeth light. But with the light there is a blessed and gracious influence, there is heat and efficacy with that light. But though a carnal man know all the body of divinity, yet it is a mere light without heat, a light without influence. It is not experimental. As a blind man can talk of colours, if he be a scholar, and describe them better than he that hath his eyes, he being

[1] There seems to be a confusion here, as if a sentence had been left out. It must be the knowledge, not of 'natural,' but of 'gracious,' men, that is as a light radicated or rooted in the soul.

not a scholar. But he that hath his eyes can judge of colours a great deal better. Oftentimes, by book, a scholar can tell you foreign countries better than he that hath travelled, yet the traveller that hath been there can tell them the more distinctly. So he that is experienced in that kind, though a stranger, can measure another man's ground better than himself. He can tell you here is so many acres. But he that possesseth them knows the goodness of them, the worth of them, and improveth them to his own good. And so it is with many. They can measure the points of religion, and define and divide them. Aye, but the poor Christian can taste, can feel them, can relish and improve them. His knowledge is a knowledge with interest, but other men's knowledge is a knowledge with no interest or experience at all. So that there is naturally a veil of ignorance on the heart of every natural man.

Christianity is a mystery. Till conversion there is a mystery in every point of religion. None know what repentance is but a repentant sinner. All the books in the world cannot inform the heart what sin is or what sorrow is. A sick man knoweth what a disease is better than all physicians, for he feeleth it. No man knoweth what faith is but the true believer. There is a mystery also in love. Godliness is called a mystery, not only for the notional, but the practical part of it. Why do not men more solace themselves in the transcendent things of religion, which may ravish angels? Alas! there is a veil over their soul, that they do not know them, or not experimentally. They have no taste or feeling of them.

And so there is a veil of unbelief. There is no man without grace that believeth truly what he knoweth; but he believeth in the general only, he believeth things so far forth as they

THE GLORIOUS FEAST OF THE GOSPEL

cross not his lusts. But when particular truths are enforced on a carnal man, his lusts do overbear all his knowledge, and he hath a secret scorn arising in his heart, whereby he derideth those truths and goeth against them, and makes him think certainly these be not true, and therefore he believeth them not. If a man by nature believed the truths he saith he knoweth, he would not go directly against them. But the ground of this is, there is a mist of sinful lusts that are raised out of the soul, that darkens the soul, that at the present time the soul is atheistical and full of unbelief. For there is no sin but ignorance and unbelief breatheth it into the soul, and maketh way for it; for if a man knew what he were about, and apprehended that God saw him, and the danger of it, he would never sin. There is no sin without an error in judgment, there is a veil of ignorance and unbelief. What creature will run into a pit when he seeth it open? What creature will run into the fire, the most dull creature? Man will not run into that danger that is open to the eye of the soul, if there were not a veil of ignorance, at least unbelief, at that time upon the soul. All sin supposeth error.

And this should make us hate sin the more. Whensoever we sin, specially against our conscience, there is atheism in the soul at that time, and there is unbelief. We believe not the truth itself. No sinner but calleth truth into question. When he sinneth, he denieth it or questioneth it; and therefore there is a veil on every man naturally over his heart by ignorance and unbelief. The truths themselves are clear. God is clear, and the gospel is light, *mens, lux*;[1] you know they know things in the object, but in us there is darkness in our understandings; and therefore the Scripture saith not

[1] Latin: *mens* = mind; *lux* = light.

we are dark only, but 'darkness itself', 2 Cor. 6:14. The clouds that arise are like the mists that do interpose between our souls and divine things, arising from our own hearts; and the love of sinful things raise such a cloud, that we know not, or else believe not, what is spoken. To proceed.

Observation 2. God only can reveal and take away the veil of ignorance and unbelief from off the soul. I will speak specially of this veil.

Reason 1. The reason is, there is such a natural unsuitableness between the soul and heavenly light and heavenly truths, that unless God opens the eye of the soul, and puts a new eye into the soul, it can never know or discern of heavenly things. There must be an eye suitable to the light, else there will never be sight of it. Now, God can create a new spiritual eye to discern of spiritual things, which a natural eye cannot. Who can see things invisible? Divine things are invisible to natural eyes. There is no suitableness. He that must reveal these and take away the veil must create new light within as well as a light without. Now, God, and only God, that created light out of darkness, can create light in the soul. 'Let there be light.' He only can create a spiritual eye, to see the things that to nature are invisible.

There be four things in sight. 1. The object to be beheld. 2. The light that conveyeth it. 3. The organ that receiveth it. 4. And the light of the eye to meet the light without. So it is in the soul. Together with divine truths, there must be light to discover them; for light is the first visible thing that discovers itself and all things else. And then there must be a light in the soul to judge of them, and this light must be suitable. A carnal, base spirit judgeth of spiritual things carnally like himself, because he hath not light in his own spirit. The things are spiritual, his eye is carnal. He hath not a light in his eye suitable to the object, and therefore he cannot judge of them, for the Scripture saith plainly 'they are spiritually discerned,' 1 Cor. 2:14. Therefore, a carnal person hath carnal conceptions of spiritual things, as a holy man doth spiritualise things by a spiritual conception of them.

There be degrees of discerning things. The highest degree is to see things 'face to face' as they be in heaven; the next to that is to see them in a glass, for there I see the motion and true species of a man, though not so clearly, as when I see him face to face; therefore we soon forget the species of it in a glass. We have more fixedness of the other, because there is more reality. We see things put into water, and that is less; but then there is a sight of man in pictures which is less than the rest, because we see not the motion. It is even so; a carnal man scarce sees the dead resemblance of things. In Moses' time they saw things in water, as it were blindly, though true; but we see things in a glass of truth as clearly as possibly we can in this world. In heaven we shall see face to face, shall see him as he is. And then will be the joy of this excellent feast, and the consummation of all sweet promises, which here we can but have a taste of.

Reason 2. So that is the first reason of it, that God is only[1] the taker away of the veil, which ariseth from the unsuitableness between the soul and divine truths.

There is nothing in the heart of man but a contrariety to divine light. The very natural knowledge, that is contrary. Natural conscience, that only checketh for gross sins, but

[1] That is, 'God only is.'

not for spiritual sins. Obedience and civil life, that makes a man full of pride, and armeth him against self-denial and against the righteousness of Christ and justification. There is nothing in the soul but, without grace, riseth against the soul in divine things.

Reason 3. Again, there is such disproportion between the soul, being full of sin and guiltiness, and heavenly things, that are so great, that the heart of man will not believe unless God convinceth the soul, that God is so good and gracious, though they be great and excellent, yet God will bestow them upon our souls; and therefore he sendeth the Spirit, that overpowers the soul, though it be full of fear and guilt that sin contracts.

Though we be never so unworthy, he will magnify his grace to poor sinners; and without that the soul will never believe there is such an infinite disproportion between the soul and the things, between the sinful soul and the Spirit, so that God must overpower the soul to make it believe.

The Scripture is full of this. As we are naturally ignorant and full of unbelief, so God only can overpower the soul and take away the veil of ignorance.

Reason 4. *All the angels in heaven, and all the creatures in the world, the most skilful men in the world, cannot bring light into the soul, they cannot bring light into the heart.* They can speak of divine things, but they understand them little. But to bring light into the heart, that the heart may taste of them and yield obedience to believe, that they cannot do. And therefore, all God's children, they be *theodidactoi*,[1] taught of God. God only hath the privilege to teach the heart, to bend and bow the heart to believe.

[1] That is, θεοδιδακτοι. Cf. John 6:45; 1 Thess. 4:9.

So that God only by his Spirit takes away the veil of ignorance and unbelief.

Observation. 3. Now, the third thing is, that this is peculiar to the church and to the children of God, to have the veil taken off. 'In this mountain,' saith the Scripture, 'the veil of all faces shall be swallowed up or taken away.'

I partly shewed in the former point, that it is peculiar to God's children to have the veil taken off. There is a veil in all things. Either the things be hid from them, as amongst the Gentiles, or if the things be revealed, there is a veil upon the heart; their lusts raise up a cloud, which, until God subdue by the Holy Spirit, they be dark, yea, darkness itself. Goshen was only light when all Egypt was in darkness; so there is light only in the church, and all other parts in the world are in darkness. And amongst men in the church there is a darkness upon the soul of unregenerate men, that be not sanctified and subdued by the Spirit of God. And all godly men are lightsome, nay, they be 'lights in the world,' Phil. 2:15. As wicked men are darkness, so gracious men, by the Spirit of God, are made lights of the world from him that is the true light, Christ himself.

It is peculiar to the church to know the greatest good, and the greatest evil. It is nowhere but in the church, who are the people of God. None but God's elect can know the greatest evil, that is, sin, which the Spirit of God revealeth; and the greatest good, that is, God's mercy in Christ, and sanctifying grace. The same Spirit doth both. As light doth discover foul things as well as fair; so the same Spirit of God discovers the loathsomeness of sin, and the sweetness of grace. Where the one is not, there is never the other; where there is not truly a deep discerning of sin, there is never knowledge of grace; there is none but in the church. Those that have the spirit of illumination, they have sanctification likewise.

We shall make use of all together. You see, then, what naturally we are, and that God's grace must take away the veil; and this is from all them within the church, and in the church those whom God is pleased to sanctify.

Observation 4. In the fourth place. *Where this veil is taken off from any, there is with it spiritual joy and feasting,* as here he joineth them both together. 'I will make a feast of fat things, and will take away the veil,' verse 7.

Reason: The reason of the connection of this, is, that same Spirit that is a Spirit of revelations, is a Spirit of comfort; and the same Spirit that is the Spirit of comfort, is a Spirit of revelation. All sweetness that the soul relisheth cometh from light, and all light that is spiritual conveyeth sweetness, both together. Beloved, there is a marvellous sweetness in divine truths. In Christ is all marrow, and in religion forgiveness of sins, and inward peace, and joy, and grace, fitting us to be like to Christ, and for heaven. They be incredibly sweet, they be all marrow. Aye, but they are only so to them that know them. Now God's Spirit, that revealeth these things to us, doth breed a taste in the soul. The Spirit of illumination to God's children, is a Spirit of sanctification likewise; and that sanctification alters the taste and relish of the will and affections, that with discovery of these things, there is a taste and relish of them. It is *sapida scientia*, a savoury knowledge they have. And therefore where he maketh a feast, he taketh away the veil;

and where he takes away the veil, he makes a feast. What a wonderful satisfaction hath the soul, when the veil is taken off, to see God in Christ reconciled! to see sin pardoned! to see the beginnings of grace, which shall be finished and accomplished in glory! to discern that 'peace which passeth understanding,' etc., Phil. 4:7. What a marvellous sweetness is in these things!

They cannot be revealed to the knowledge spiritually, but there is a feast in the soul, wherein the soul doth solace itself; so both these go together.

And therefore we should not rest in that revealing that doth not bring a savour with it to the soul. Undoubtedly, that knowledge hath no solace and comfort for the soul, that is not by divine revelation of heavenly truths.

We see the dependence of these one upon another. Then let us make this use of all:

Use 1. Since there is a veil over all men by nature, the work of ignorance and unbelief, and since God only taketh it away by his Holy Spirit, and since that only those that be godly and sanctified have this taken off: while this is, there is a spiritual feast, joy, and comfort, and strength; then *let us labour to have this veil taken off; let us labour to have the eyes of our understandings enlightened, to have our hearts subdued to believe; let us take notice of our natural condition.* We are drowned and enwrapt in darkness, the best of all. It is not having knowledge what we are by nature; it is not any knowledge that can bring us to heaven; there must be a revelation, a taking away of the veil. How many content themselves with common light of education, and traditionary knowledge! So they were bred and catechised, and under such a ministry! But for spiritual knowledge of spiritual things, how little is it cared for! And yet this is necessary to salvation. There is great occasion to press this, that we rest not in common knowledge. If religion be not known to purpose, it is like lightning, which directs not a man in his way, but dazzles him, and puts him quite out of his way. Many have flashes of knowledge that affect them a little; but this affection is soon gone, and directs them not a whit in the ways of life. And therefore labour that the will and affections may be subject. Beg of God a 'fleshy heart,' 2 Cor. 3:3, an heart yielding to the truth. We know ear-truths will harden, as none is harder than a common formal Christian. A man had better fall into the hands of papists, than into the hands of a formal hypocritical Christian. Why? They pride themselves in their profession. No persecutors worse than the Scribes and Pharisees, that stood in their own light. They were more cruel than Pilate. And therefore if we be informed, but not truly transformed, to love the truth we know, and hate the evil we know, it maketh us worse.

And then it enrageth men the more. The more they know, the more they be enraged. Men, when truths be pressed, which they purpose not to obey, they fret against the ordinance, and cast stones, as it were, in the face of truth. When physic[1] doth raise humours, but is not strong enough to carry them away, they endanger the body; and where light is not strong enough to dispel corruption when it raiseth corruption, it enrageth it. When men know truth, and are not moulded into it, they first rage against it, and then by little and little fall from it, and grow extreme enemies to it.

[1] That is, medicine.

It is a dangerous thing, therefore, to rest in naked knowledge. Beg then of God that he would take away the veil of ignorance and unbelief, that light and life may go together, and so we shall be fit to feast with the Lord.

Means. Now that we may have true saving knowledge, first, *we must attend meekly upon God's ordinances*, which be sanctified to this end to let in light to the soul.

1. Will we know sin and our state by nature, and how to come out of it; then together with this revelation *must come an heavenly strength into the soul, a heavenly taste and relish*; and therefore attend upon the ordinances, and labour for an humble soul, empty of ourselves; and do not think to break into heavenly things with strength of parts. God must reveal, God must take away the veil only by his Holy Spirit in the ordinance. The veil is taken away from the object, in opening of truths; but the veil must be taken away from the object, and from the heart too. There must be knowledge of the object, as well as an object. The object must be sanctified and fitted to the persons, else divine truths will never be understood divinely, nor spiritual truths spiritually. Labour to be emptied of yourselves. In what measure we are emptied of our self-conceitedness and understanding, we be filled in divine things. In what measure we are emptied of ourselves, we are filled with the Spirit of God, and knowledge, and grace. As a vessel, in what measure it is emptied, in that measure it is fit to be filled with more supervenient liquor; so in what measure we grow in self-denial and humility, in that measure we are filled likewise with knowledge. He will teach an humble soul that stands not in its own light, what it is to

repent, to believe, to love; what it is to be patient under the cross; what it is to live holily, and die comfortably. The Spirit of God will teach an humble, self-denying soul all these things; and therefore labour for an humble, empty soul, and not to cast ourselves too much into the sins and fashions of the times, as the apostle, 'Be not conformed to this world, but be ye transformed by the renewing of your mind,' etc., Rom. 12:2.

2. *When a man casteth himself into the mould of the times, and will live as the rest do, he shall never understand the secrets of God, and the good pleasure of God*; for the world must be condemned. The world goeth the broad way. And therefore we must not consider what others do, but what God teacheth us to do.

3. And add to this, *what we know, let us labour to practise.* 'But he that doth the will of my Father, shall know of every doctrine, whether it be of God or no,' John 7:17. We must do, and we shall know.

Question. But can we do before we know?

Answer. The meaning is this, that we have, first, breeding and education, and some light of the Spirit turneth it presently to practice, by obedience to that knowledge. And then you shall know more. He that doth these things, he shall know all. They shall know that do practise what they know already. 'To him that hath shall be given,' Matt. 13:12; that is, to him that hath some knowledge, and putteth in practice what he hath, God will increase the talent of his knowledge; he shall know more and more, till God revealeth himself fully in the world to come.

4. And therefore *be faithful to ourselves, and true to the knowledge we have, love it*, and put it into practice. When

divine truths are discovered, let the heart affect them, lest God giveth us up to believe lies. We have many given up to this sin. Because when truths are revealed, they give way to their own proud scornful hearts, they know not the love of the truth. God knoweth what a jewel the truth is; and since they despise it, God giveth them up to believe lies. And take heed, practise what we know, and love what we know, entertain it with a loving affection.

A loving affection is the casket of this jewel. If we entertain it not in love, it removes from us its station, and being gone, God will remove us into darkness.

And remember it is God that taketh away the veil of ignorance and unbelief. And therefore make this use of it.

Use 2. To make our studies and closets, oratories,[1] not to come to divine truths, to out-wrestle the excellency of them with our own wits; but to pray to God, as you have Psa. 119:18, 'Open mine eyes, and reveal thy truth.' And St Paul prayeth for the 'spirit of revelation,' Eph. 1:17. And so desire God to reveal and take away the veil from us, that he will open divine truths to our souls; that since he hath the key of David, that 'opens, and no man shutteth,' Rev. 3:7, that he would open our understandings to conceive things, and our hearts to believe. He hath the only key of the soul. We can shut our souls, but cannot open them again. So we can shut our hearts to divine truths, we can naturally do this; but open them without the help of the Spirit we cannot. He can open our understandings, as he did the disciples'. He can open our hearts to believe; he can do it, and will do it. If we seek to him, he will not put back the humble

[1] That is, 'places of prayer.'

desires of them that fear him. And therefore for heavenly light and heavenly revelation, all the teaching of the men of the world cannot do it. If we know no more than we can have by books, and men that teach us, we shall never come to heaven; but we must have God teach the heart, as well as the brain. He must teach not only the truths themselves, as they be discovered, but the love of them, the faith in them, the practice of them; and he only can do this, he only can teach the heart, he only can discover the bent of the heart, and Satan's wiles that cast a cloud upon the understanding. The Spirit only can do it; and therefore in all our endeavours, labour to get knowledge, and join holiness and divine grace, and pray to God that he would reveal the mystery of salvation to us.

Question. But how shall we know whether we have this heavenly light and revelation or no? whether the veil be yet upon our hearts or no? I will not be long in the point.

Answer 1. We may know it by this. The apostle Peter saith to express the virtue of God's power, 'He hath called us out of darkness to his marvellous light,' 1 Pet. 2:9. The soul that hath the veil taken from it, *there is a marvelling at the goodness of God, a wondering at the things of faith.* And the soul sets such a price upon divine things, that all is 'dung and dross' in comparison of the excellent knowledge of Jesus Christ, Phil. 3:8. Wherefore is it that thou wilt reveal thyself to us, and not unto the world? as admiring the goodness of God. What are we? What am I, that God should reveal these things to me, and not to the world? that many perish in darkness and shadow of death, though they hear of divine things, yet they, teaching rebellion and unbelief, are not moulded to them, and so perish eternally? There is a secret admiration of the goodness of God to the poor soul, and a wonderment at spiritual things. 'O! how sweet is thy law,' saith David, Psa. 119:103. And teach me the wonders of thy law, and joy unspeakable and glorious, and peace that passeth understanding, Phil. 4:7. These things be high to the soul.

Answer 2. By the taste of what they have, they wonder at that little, and at that they look for, *and are carried with desire still further and further, which is a farther evidence.* They that have any spiritual knowledge, they be carried to grow more and more, and to enter further and further into the kingdom. Where there is not a desire still, till they come to the full measure that is to be had in Jesus Christ, there is no knowledge at all. Certainly a gracious soul, when once it sees, it desires still to feel the power and virtue of Christ in it, as Paul counted all dung in comparison of this knowledge, to know myself in Christ, and feel the power of his death in dying to sin, and virtue of his resurrection in raising me to newness of life. It was Saint Paul's study to walk still to the high prize of God's calling, and where that is not, no grace is begun.

Answer 3. And again, where divine light is, and the veil taken away, *it is the sanctified means;* for God works by his own instruments and means, and they be able to justify all courses of wisdom. 'Wisdom is justified of her children,' Matt. 11:19. By experience they be able to say the word is the word. I have found it casting me down, and raising me up, and searching the hidden corners of my heart. I have found God's ordinances powerful, the word and sacrament. I have found my hope, faith, strength, and spiritual comfort, and therefore I can justify them; for I have found, tasted, and relished of these things, which worketh that upon the soul which Christ did on the body. I find mine eyes, I find my deaf ears opened. I can hear with another relish than before. I find a life and quickening to good things, though it be weak. I had no life at all to them before. I find a relish which I knew not before. So that there be spiritual senses whereby I am able to justify that these things be the things of God. So that they that have divine truths can justify all the ordinances of God by their own experience. As Peter answered when Christ asked him, Will you be also gone? Be gone! said Peter; 'Whither should we go? thou hast the words of eternal life,' John 6:68. I have found thy words efficacious to comfort and strengthen and raise, and shall I depart from thee, who hast the words of eternal life? And so take a soul that the Spirit of God hath wrought upon. Ask whether they will be careless of means of salvation, not to pray, or hear, or receive the sacrament. By these have I eternal life conveyed. God hath let in by these comfort, and strength, and joy, and shall I leave these things? No; I will not. 'Whither shall I go? thou hast the words of eternal life.' Are we able to justify these things by the sweetness we have found in them? Then certainly God hath shined upon the soul, and, together with strength and light, conveyed sweetness to the soul.

Answer 4. A godly man *seeth things with life, his sight worketh upon him*. It is a transforming sight. As the apostle saith, 'We all behold the glory of God, and are changed,' 2 Cor. 3:18. Sight of light and life goeth together with a Christian; as Christ saith, 'he is the light of the world,' John 9:5, and 'the life of the world,' John 1:4. First light, for life cometh with light, and light conveyeth life. All grace is dropped into the will through the understanding; and wheresoever Christ is life, he is light, because true knowledge is a transforming knowledge. But if religion be not known to purpose, it hardens and makes worse.

We are now by God's good providence come to farther business, to partake of these mysteries;[1] yet it should be the desire of our souls that our eyes may be opened, that in these divine and precious mysteries he would discover hidden love, which is not seen with the eyes of the body. They may see and taste and relish his love and goodness in Jesus Christ; that as the outward man is refreshed with the elements, so the inward man may be refreshed with his Spirit, that they may be effectual to us; that we may justify the course God takes, so far as to come charitably and joyfully to them.

[1] In the margin, 'Application of this to the sacrament.'

Sermon 4

*I will destroy in this mountain the face of the covering cast
over all people, and the veil that is spread over all nations.
He will swallow up death in victory, etc.*

– Isaiah 25:7, 8

WE have heretofore at large spoken of the spiritual and
eternal favours of God, set out in the former verse, 'In this
mountain will the Lord of hosts make a feast of fat things.'
While our soul is in the body, it is much guided by our
fancy. Spiritual things are therefore presented by outward,
and conveyed to the soul that way; only we must remember
that there is a far greater excellency in the things themselves than in their representation. For what is all banquets,
fatness with marrow, wine on the lees, to the joy and sweetness of religion, begun here, and accomplished in the world
to come?

In Christ there is nothing but all marrow and sweetness
in religion, that may refresh a man in the lowest condition,
if he can but have a taste of it. Now because the spiritual
things of Christ do us no good, as long as they are hid,
therefore the Holy Ghost setteth down a promise, 'that God
will take away the covering cast on all people, and the veil
spread over all nations.'

But there be some things that will damp all mirth. Now
here is security against them, that our joy may be complete;

and this in the next verse, to which I now come, 'He will swallow up death in victory, he will wipe away tears from all faces.' The prophet having spoken of a great feast before, an excellent feast, sets forth here the services of that feast. What is it that accompanies it?

First of all, there shall be light to discover the excellency of the feast; the veil is taken away, and a knowledge given to know divine things in a spiritual manner.

Then, which will damp all feasts, the fear of death is taken away. 'He will swallow up death in victory, and wipe away all tears,' that is, all sorrow. The effect is put for the cause. This is an excellent promise, an excellent service in this spiritual banquet. Suppose a man were set at a feast furnished with all delicates, royally attended, clothes suitable, and had a sword hung over his head ready to fall upon him, it would cast such a damp on his spirit, as would spoil the joy of this feast. So to hear of spiritual excellencies, and yet death, and hell, and damnation coming along, alas! where is the comfort you speak of. And therefore to make the feast more perfect, there is not only light and knowledge, but removal of it ever may damp the feast. So this must needs come in to comfort all the rest. 'He shall swallow up death in victory, and wipe away tears from all faces.' Death is here represented to us under the word victory, as a combatant, as one that we are to fight withal, a captain.

And then here is the victory of him, Christ overcomes him, and overcomes him gloriously. It is not only a conquest, but a swallowing of him up. Usually God useth all sorts of enemies in their own kind. He causeth them that spoil to be spoiled, them that swallow up to be swallowed up. So death the great swallower shall be swallowed up.

Beloved, death is the great king of kings, and the emperor of emperors, the great captain and ruling king of the world; for no king hath such dominion as death hath. It spreads its government and victory over all nations. He is equal, though a tyrant. As a tyrant spares none, he is equal in this. He subdueth young and old, poor and rich. He levels sceptres and spades together. He levels all. There is no difference between the dust of an emperor and the meanest man. He is a tyrant that governeth over all. And so there is this equity in him, he spares none.

He hath continued from the beginning of the world to this time; but he is a tyrant brought in by ourselves, Rom. 5:19, *seq*. Sin let in death. It opened the door. Death is no creature of God's making. Satan brought in sin, and sin brought in death. So that we be accessory ourselves to the powerful stroke of this prevailing tyrant. And therefore sin is called the cause of death. Sin brought in death, and armeth death. The weapon that death fights with, and causeth great terror, it is sin. The cause is armed with the power of the wrath of God for sin, the fear of hell, and damnation. So that wrath, and hell, and damnation, arming sin, it bringeth a sting of itself, and puts a venom into death. All cares, and fears, and sorrows, and sicknesses, are less and petty deaths, harbingers to death itself; but the attendants that follow this great king are worst of all, as Rev. 6:8, 'I saw a pale horse, and death upon it, and after him comes hell.' What were death, if it were not for the pit, and dungeon that followeth it? So that death is attended with hell, and hell with eternity.

Therefore here is a strange kind of prevailing. There is no victory where there is no enemy, and therefore death must needs be an enemy, yea, it is the worst enemy, and the last enemy. Death is not planted in the forlorn hope, but it is planted at last for the greatest advantage, and is a great enemy. What doth death? It depriveth us of all comfort, pleasure, communion with one another in this life, callings or whatsoever else is comfortable. The grave is the house of oblivion. Death is terrible of itself, even to nature, as Augustine saith, where it is not swallowed up of Christ; for it is an evil in itself, and as I said, armed with a sting of sin, after which follows hell.

Now this death is swallowed up. When the Scripture puts a person upon death,[1] it is not uncomely for us to speak as the Scripture doth. The Scripture puts a person upon death, and a kind of triumphing spirit in God's children over death. 'O death, where is thy sting? O grave, where is thy victory?' 1 Cor. 15:55. Death is the greatest swallower, and yet it is swallowed up by Christ. Death hath swallowed up all, and when it hath swallowed up, it keepeth them. It keeps the dust of kings, subjects, great and small, to the general day of judgment, when death shall be swallowed up of itself. It is therefore of the nature of those that Solomon speaks of, that cry, 'Give, give,' Prov. 30:15, and yet is never satisfied, like the grave, yet this death is swallowed up in victory.

But how cometh death to be swallowed up? Christ will swallow up death in victory, for himself and his.

Reason. First of all, because sin brought in death, our Saviour Christ became sin, a sacrifice to his Father's justice for sin. He was made sin for us, he was made a curse for us,

---

[1] That is, 'personifies.'

to take away the curse due to us; and sin being taken away, what hath death to do with us, and hell, and damnation, the attendants on death? Nothing at all. Therefore, Col. 2:14, upon the cross Christ did nail the law, and sin, and the devil. There he reigned over principalities and powers, which were but executioners let loose by reason of our sins. And God being satisfied for sin, the devil hath nothing to do with us, but to exercise us, except it be for our good. So that he hath swallowed up death, because by his death he hath taken away sin, and so the power of Satan, whose power is by sin. And therefore it is excellently set down, Heb. 2:14, 'He also took part of flesh and blood, that through death he might destroy him that had the power of death, that is, the devil.' So Christ by death overthrew Satan, that had the power of death, because by death he took away sin, the sins of all, and bore our sins upon the cross, and was made sin for us, that knew no sin. He is ours, if we believe. For then Christ is given to a particular man when he believes. Beloved, Christ upon the cross did triumph over all our spiritual enemies, sin, and death, and all. It was a kingdom of patience. You know there is a double kingdom of Christ; a kingdom of patience, and a kingdom of power.

1. Christ on the cross suffering punishment due to sin, overcame the law, and the devil, and sin, which is the kingdom of patience.

2. The kingdom of power he hath in heaven. If Christ were so able in his kingdom of patience to conquer our greatest enemies, what will he do in his kingdom of power? As Paul reasoneth, 'If by his death we are saved, much more now he triumphs in heaven, and appears for us, is he able to convey greater matters to us,' Rom. 5:21.

If Christ in the days of his flesh did conquer, how glorious will his conquest be at the day of judgment! Now, Christ hath conquered all in his own person, as our head; then he will conquer for us in his mystical body. What is now done in his person, shall be done in his members. In the meantime, faith is our victory, his conquest over death our victory; his victory over all our spiritual enemies is our victory. Every one that believeth is a conqueror of death, though he die, because he sees it conquered in Christ his head; and as it is truly conquered in him, so Christ will conquer it in all his members. For as Christ in his natural body is gone to heaven, there to appear in our behalf, so shall mystical Christ be wholly in glory. He will not leave a finger. We shall all triumph over all our spiritual enemies. As Christ's natural body is glorious in heaven as our head, so shall also his mystical body be.

You see then how death is swallowed up by Christ as our surety, as the second Adam upon the cross; and truly swallowed up in him. And by faith this victory is ours, and time will come when in our own persons it shall be swallowed up in victory.

This might be enlarged, but I haste to make use of it.

Mark, I beseech you, how death is swallowed up by Christ in his own person for our good. He gave a great way to death, for death seized on him upon the cross. Death severeth soul from body. Death had him in his own cabinet, his grave, for three days. Nay, this great king and tyrant death, had a great conquest over Christ himself. But here was the glory of this victory! When death, this great conqueror of the world, had Christ upon the cross, and in his own dominion, in the grave, where he rules and reigns, consuming and swallowing up all, death was fain to give up all; and Satan thought to have had a great morsel when he devoured Christ, but there was an hook in his divine power that catched him, that when he thought to have swallowed up Christ, was swallowed up himself. His head was then broken. He never had such a blow, as by Christ on the cross, when he was overcome, being a scorn of the world visibly, yet invisibly in God's acceptation of that sacrifice, and in a spirit of faith. Christ triumpheth over Satan. Death was subdued even in his own kingdom, and that makes the victory great.

Death by seizing on Christ without right, Christ hath freed us from the evil of death when it had right to us. Death hath lost all its right by fastening on Christ, and so is become as a drone[1] without a sting. So the great swallower of all is swallowed up itself at last by Christ.

Use 1. Now for comfortable use of it. First, let us consider *that God oftentimes giveth a great deal of way to his greatest enemies.* God useth a stratagem of retiring; he seems to retire and give liberty to his enemies, but it is to triumph and trample upon them with greater shame. He will tread them to dust afterward. Christ gave death a great deal of liberty. He was crucified and tormented, then had[2] to the grave, and there he lay. And this was to raise a greater triumph over this great prevailer, over the world and death itself.

It is continued so in the church. Doth not he give way to the enemies of the church? They may come to say, Aha,

[1] That is, the 'drone' bee.
[2] That is, 'taken.'

aha, so would we have it. Now the poor children of God are where we would have them, but then comes sudden destruction. God, to make his victory more glorious, and more to discover their cruelty, comes upon them when they be in the top of pleasure, and the church in the bottom of abasement. Then God swalloweth up all in victory, as Christ did death when it seemed to have been itself victorious.

This is a very comfortable consideration, for if death be overcome when it seemed to overcome Christ, what need we fear any other enemy? Christ hath broken the net, as an eagle or great bird, and the rest escape by him.

You may enlarge this in your own meditations. He will swallow up death in victory. This is said for the time to come, he will swallow up death. But Paul saith it is also past, and swallowed up already. Faith saith it is done; and so it is in our head. Were it not comfortable now to all true-hearted Christians, to hear that the church fareth better, and that the enemies were swallowed up, for they be but the instruments of this inferior death? Let us get the spirit of faith, and see them all conquered, for certainly they shall have the worst at last. He that hath swallowed up death in victory, will swallow up all that be the cause of death. And therefore the Scripture speaks of these things as past, 'Babylon is fallen, as a millstone cast into the bottom of the sea,' Rev. 18:21.

Get a spirit of faith, and we shall never be much troubled with Babylon; for all the enemies of Christ, and adherents to that man of sin, must down, and partake of the judgments threatened in the Revelations. Heaven hath concluded it, and all the policy of Rome and hell cannot disannul it. They be already swallowed up to faith, and Christ will rule till he hath put them all under his feet, Psa. 110:1; which shall be done, not only to destroy them, but to raise himself higher, in giving them up to their confusion.

Use 2. Again, if death be swallowed up in victory, labour to be one with Christ crucified, for union with him. Begin with union with Christ crucified. The first union is with Christ abased, and then with Christ glorified. And therefore labour to see sin, that brought in death, subdued by the power of Christ's death in some measure, and then we shall have comfort in his death glorified. For in my 'holy mount' death is swallowed up, that is, the true church of Christ. Labour to be members of Christ, otherwise death will come as a tyrant indeed, armed with a terrible sting, in his full force to assail you. It is the most terrible thing to see death come armed with the wrath and anger of God, and attended with hell and damnation. Labour, therefore, to be one with Christ crucified, to get our sins crucified, and ourselves partakers of his death; and then no damnation, no fear of death to them that are in Christ. They may die, but they are freed from eternal death, and they shall rise again, even as Christ's body rose, to glory.

Get, therefore, into Christ, and desire the power of his death subduing sin. In what measure we grow in that, we grow in boldness and joy, and whatsoever privileges follow Christ.

Use 3. Again, when we be in Christ, true members of him, then *let us be thankful to God for this victory, thankful to Jesus Christ that hath given us victory*. When we think of death, of sin, of judgment, of hell, of damnation, let us be framed as a Christian should. Now let him that hath the most terrible and fearful things in the world as conquered enemies, say, Oh, blessed be God for Christ, and blessed be Christ for dying for us, and by death disarming death of his sting! That now we can think of it in our judgments quietly; now we can think of all these as conquered enemies: this is the fruit of Christ's death. They are not only enemies, but friends in Christ. Sin, the remainder of it – (the guilt of it, that bindeth over to damnation, is taken away) – the remainders of it serve to humble us, make us feel the power of pardon, and to desire another world, where we shall be all spiritual. So that death is a part of our jointure. 'All things are yours, life and death,' 1 Cor. 3:22. Death doth us many excellent services. It is a door and passage to life. Death is the death of itself, destroyeth itself. We never truly live till we die, and when we die, we are past fear of death. So that sin dieth, misery dieth, death dieth. Though it takes us from comforts, and employments, and friends here, yet it is a change to a better place, and better company, and better employments, and better condition, to be in a glorious condition to eternity; and therefore we have cause to bless God in Christ, that took our nature, and in our nature disarmed our greatest enemy, sin, and so disarmed death, and freed us from the wrath of God, and hell, and damnation. Oh, we can never be thankful enough for this!

Use 4. Again, if death be swallowed up in victory, *let us be ashamed of the fear of death*, because Christ saith he will swallow him up, as he hath already in his own person. Shall we be afraid of an enemy that is swallowed up in our head, and shall be swallowed up in every one of us? If we cherish fear, we shew we look not for an interest in this promise; for it is a promise, that 'in this holy mountain death shall be swallowed up in victory,' and why should we fear a conquered enemy? None will fear an enemy that is conquered.

Objection. But how came Christ to fear death, and we not to fear?

Answer. Christ had to deal with death armed with a terrible sting, with sin, and the wrath of God for sin. And, therefore, when he was to die, 'Father, let this cup pass from me,' Matt. 26:39. But death is disarmed to us. He had to encounter with sin and the wrath of God, and death in all its strength. But we are not so. We are to deal with death like the brazen serpent, that hath the shape of death, but no sting at all. It has become a drone ever since it lost its sting in Christ. Life took death, that death might take life, as he said. The meaning is, Christ's life itself took death, that we that were so subject to death, that we were death itself, might take life. Oh blessed consideration! Nothing comparable to the consideration of the death of Christ! It is the death of death.

And then again we are sure of victory. It is conquered in our head, and shall be in us. But you say we are to conflict with the pangs of death, and many troubles meet in death. It is true, but it is conquered to faith, and in Christ our head. We must fight. Christ traineth us to overcome death ourselves by faith, and then we are sure of victory. Join these two together. It is conquered in Christ our head, and shall be conquered of us. Death keeps our dust, and must give them all again.

Objection. But in the meantime we die.

Answer. 'Tis so, but we are sure of victory. He will protect us in our combat, that hath conquered for us. We fight against death and the terror of it, in the strength and faith of his victory. Join these three together.

He that hath been our Saviour in life, will be so to death, and not exclusively, then to leave us, but to death, and in death, forever; yea, most ready to help us in our last conflict. Indeed, to wicked men death is terrible, for he sendeth the devil to fetch them out of the world; but for those that be his, he sendeth his angels to fetch them, and he helps them in their combat. We must not therefore fear over much. There is a natural fear of death. Death wrought upon Christ himself, God-man; not only death, but such a death. He was to be left of his Father, and lie under the sense of the wrath of God; the separation of that soul from the body he took upon him was terrible; and therefore he saith, 'If it be possible, let this cup pass from me': that was nature, and without it he had not been true man. But that I say is, that grace may be above nature. Death is a time of darkness. It strips us of earthly comforts, friends, callings, employments; but then comes the eye of faith to lay hold of the victory on Christ in time to come, when death shall be only swallowed up in victory; and then the glorious state to come, to which death bringeth us. So that here faith must be above sense, and grace above nature, and therefore I beseech you, let us labour for it.

There be two sorts of men to whom I would speak a little.

First. Those that in a kind of bravery seem to slight death; men of base spirits, as we call them; fools, vain-glorious spirits, empty spirits. Is there any creature, unless in Christ, able groundedly[1] to slight so great an enemy as death, armed with a sting of sin, and attended with hell and damnation? The Romish and devilish spirits are terrible; but if thy sins be not pardoned, it is the most terrible thing in the world to die, for there is a gulf afterwards. What shall we say, then, of single combatants, that for vain glory are prodigal of their lives, that for a foul word, a little disgrace, will venture on this enemy, that is armed with sin, and if they die, they die in sin.[2] And which is the miserable condition of him that dies in sin: his death opens the gate to another death, which is eternal. They say they have repented, but there is no repentance of a sin to be committed. Canst thou repent of a sin before it be committed? that is but a mockery of God. And what saith the Scripture? Is it not the most terrible judgment under heaven to die in our sins? A man that dies in sin dies in hell: he goeth from death to hell, and that eternal.

I wonder, therefore, that the wisdom of flesh and blood should take away men's wit, and faith, and grace, and all, so much as to slight death, and repentance, as if it were so easy. Now, beloved, death is a terrible thing. It hath a sting, and thou shalt know it. If thou hast not grace to feel the sting of it whilst thou livest, when thou diest the sting will revive; then thy conscience shall awake in hell. Drunkenness and jollity take away sense of sin; but sin will revive, and conscience will revive. God hath not put it into us for nought. Death is terrible, if not disarmed beforehand. And if thou go about to die without disarming it before, it will not be outfaced. It is not an enemy to be scorned and

[1] That is, 'on good grounds.'
[2] In the margin, 'of [the] duellist.'

slighted. And, therefore, be Christians in good earnest, else leave profession, and perish eternally. For we must all die; and it is a greater matter than we take it. But if we be true Christians, it is the sweetest thing in the world, an end of all misery, a beginning of true happiness, an inlet to whatsoever is comfortable. Blessed are they that are in the Lord by faith, and them that die in the Lord. Their death is better than the day of life. Our birthday brings us into misery; and therefore let me speak to true Christians, and bid them be ashamed of fearing death too much, which, of an enemy is become a reconciled friend.

Second. This may in the next place yield great consolation to those that are in Christ Jesus, that death by Christ is swallowed up in victory; and the rather, because the Holy Ghost meaneth more than a bare victory over death. Death is not only subdued, but is made a friend to us, as Psa. 110:1, it is said 'his enemies shall be his footstool.' Now a footstool is not only trampled upon, but an help to rise. And so death is not only subdued, but it advanceth God's children, and raiseth them higher. It is not only an enemy, but a reconciled friend; for he doth that which no friend in the world can do. It ends all our misery, and is the inlet into all happiness for eternity. And whatsoever it strips us of here, it giveth us advantage of better in another world. It cuts off our pleasures, and profits, and company, and callings here; but what is that to our blessed change afterward, to our praying of God forever, to the company of blessed souls, and the profits, and pleasures at the right hand of God for evermore? And therefore it is not only conquered, but to shew the excellency of his power, he hath made it a friend of an enemy, and the best friend in the world. It indeed separates from body, but it joineth the soul to Christ; so that the conjunction we have by it is better than the separation, if the conjunction makes us partake of our desire. 'I desire to be dissolved,' saith St Paul, Phil. 1:28, but that is not well translated. 'I desire to *depart*, and to be with Christ, which is best of all.' So that it is not only not an enemy, but a friend. And therefore the apostle makes it our jointure,[1] part of our portion, all things are yours. Why? 'You are Christ's, and Christ is God's,' 1 Cor. 3:22. What are ours? 'Things present, things to come, life, death,' 1 Cor. 3:22, 23. And well may death be ours, because sin is our enemy; that remainder, that is kept in our nature to exercise us, and humble us, and fit us for grace. As Augustine saith, I dare be bold to say, it is profitable for some to fall, to make them more careful and watchful, and to prize mercy more. So that not only death, but sin and the devil himself is ours; for his plots are for our good. God over-shooteth him in his own bow. 'He will give them over to Satan,' saith the apostle, 'that they may learn not to blaspheme,' 1 Tim. 1:20. Yet though they have a spirit of blasphemy by the humbling of their bodies, they be taught not to blaspheme; so that not only death, but sin, and he that brought sin into the world, the devil, are become our friends.

This being so, it may be for special comfort that we fear not the king of fears. The devil hath great advantage by this affection of fear, when it is set upon this object death. Overcome death, and all troubles are overcome. Who will fear anything that hath given up himself to God? 'Skin for skin, and all that a man hath, will he give for his life,' Job

---

[1] Jointure = an estate settled on a wife.

2:4. The devil knoweth that well enough. Therefore 'fear not,' saith Christ, 'them that can kill the body,' Matt. 10:28. Fear causeth snares, saith Solomon, Prov. 29:25, snares of conscience. But if a man hath overcome the fear of death once, what more is to be done? What if they take away life, they cannot take away that that is better than life, the favour of God. If we die in the Lord, we die in the favour of God, which is better than life; and we shall be found in the Lord at the day of judgment, and shall be forever with the Lord in heaven; and therefore this is a ground of resolution in good causes, notwithstanding all threats whatsoever, because death itself is swallowed up in victory.

The worst the world can do is to take away this nature of ours. When they have done that, they have done all they can; and when they have done that, they have done a pleasure. That is not to be feared, saith Tertullian, that frees us from all that is to be feared.[1] What is to be feared in the world? Every sickness, every disgrace? Why, death frees us from all. We do see every day takes away a piece of one's life, and when death cometh it overthroweth itself; for the soul goeth presently to the place of happiness. The body sleepeth a while, and death hath no more power.

'He that believeth in me,' saith Christ, 'he shall not see death, but is passed from death to life,' John 5:24. He shall not see spiritual death; but as he lives in Christ, shall die in Christ, and rise again in Christ. He that hath the life of grace begun, shall have it consummate without interruption. It is a point of wonderful comfort, that death is so overcome

---

[1] 'That is not to be feared,' saith Tertullian, 'that frees us from all that is to be feared.' This is taken from Tertullian *de Testimonio Animae* ('On the Testimony of the Soul') § iv.

that we be in heaven already. And it is no hard speech, but stands with the truth of other points; for are not Christ and we all one? His body is there, and is not he the head of his mystical body? He that carried his natural body, will not he carry his mystical body thither too? will he be in piecemeal in heaven? Therefore we are in heaven already the best part of us. We are represented in heaven, for Christ represents us there as the husband doth the wife. He hath taken up heaven for us.

Christ cannot be divided, as Augustine saith. 'We sit in heavenly places already with Christ,' Eph. 1:3. And what a comfort is this, that while we live we are in heaven, and that death cannot hinder us from our resurrection, which is the restoring of all things. And therefore, as the apostle saith, 'Comfort one another with these things,' 1 Thess. 4:18. These things indeed have much comfort in them.

Let us labour then to be comfortable: this use the apostle makes of it; and fruitful in our places, upon consideration of the victory we have by Christ. 1 Cor. 15. It is an excellent chapter that largely proveth Christ's victory, as the cause of our victory, because he is the first-fruit that sanctifieth all the rest. 'Finally, my brethren, be constant, immoveable, always abounding in the works of the Lord, knowing that your labour is not in vain in the Lord.' He raiseth that exhortation of fruitfulness and constancy from this very ground of the victory Christ hath gotten by death. 'O death, where is thy sting? O grave, where is thy victory? Thanks be to God through Jesus Christ.' 'And therefore be constant, immoveable, always abounding in the work of the Lord, knowing that your labour shall not be in vain in the Lord,' 1 Cor. 15:58. Make that use the apostle doth of fruitfulness to God for Christ, that we can think of death, and sin, the devil, and all his malice, and not be afraid; yea, think of them all with comfort, that we be not only freed from their tyranny, but they be our friends.

Christ hath the key of hell and death; a saying taken from the custom of governors that carried the key. He hath the government and command of hell and death. Now if Christ hath command of death, he will not suffer death to hurt his members, or triumph always over them. He will keep them in the grave. Our bodies are safe in the grave. The dust is fitted for a heavenly, for another manner of body than we have now; and Christ that hath the key will let them out again. Therefore trust a while till times of restoring come, and then we shall have a glorious soul, and glorious body, as the apostle saith, 1 Cor. 15:43. I beseech you, think of these things, and get comfort against the evil day. And to that end, be sure to get into Christ, that we may be in Christ, living, and dying, and be found in Christ. For what saith the Scripture? 'Blessed are they that die in the Lord,' Rev. 14:13. It is an argument of blessedness to die for the Lord, but if it be not in the Lord, it is to no purpose. If there is granted this happiness of dying for the Lord, it is well; 'but blessed are they that die in the Lord.' Why? 'They rest from their labour.' Death takes them off from their labours. All their good works go to heaven with them. So saith the Spirit, whatsoever the flesh saith. And there is no resting till that time. Their life is full of troubles and combers,[1] and therefore labour to get assurance that we are in Christ, that we be in Christ, and die in Christ, and then 'there is no condemnation to them that are in Christ.'

[1] That is, 'cumbers,' cares.

How besotted are we to put away preparation of death till it comes! He that forgets Christ and getting into Christ, all his lifetime, it is God's just judgment that he should forget himself in death. We see how a villain that hath no care of his own life, may have power of another man's life.

And therefore labour to be engrafted into Christ by faith; and that we may know it by the Spirit of Christ prevailing in us over our natural corruptions more and more. As the apostle saith, 'There is no condemnation to them that are in Christ'; for the spirit of life, 'the law of the spirit of life which is in Christ, hath freed me from the law of sin and death,' Rom. 8:2, *seq.*, the condemning law of sin. If the law of the spirit of life which is in Christ the head, be in us in any measure, it frees us from the condemning law of sin, that it carrieth us not whither it would. Then we may say with comfort, 'There is no condemnation to them that are in Christ'; for the law of the spirit of life in Christ hath freed us from the condemning, tyrannizing law of sin and death.

Sin hath no law. It is in us as a subdued rebel, but it sets not up a throne. Some hope to be saved by Christ, and yet they set up sin a throne in the soul. Sin biddeth them defile themselves, and they must obey it. This is a woeful estate! How can they expect to die in the Lord, but such as are freed by the law of the spirit of life? New lords, new laws. When kings conquer, they bring fundamental laws; and when we are taken from Satan's kingdom into the kingdom of Christ, the fundamental laws are then altered. Christ by his Spirit sets up a law of believing, and praying and doing good, and abstaining from evil. The law of the spirit of life frees us from the law of sin and death.

I beseech you, enlarge these things in your thoughts. They be things we must all have use of beforehand, against the evil day. It should be comfortable and useful to us all, to hear that our enemy, our greatest enemy, death, is swallowed up in victory. And yet there is more comfort in the text.

Sermon 5

And all tears shall be wiped away from all faces.
                                                    – Isaiah 25:8

NOT only death shall be swallowed up in victory, but God 'will wipe away all tears from all eyes.' Religion shall be religion; good things shall be good things. Nothing shall go under false notions. All tears shall be wiped away. We have now many causes of tears. In the world there is continual raising of clouds, that distil into drops of tears. Had we nothing without us to raise a vapour to be distilled in tears, we are able to raise up mists from our own mists, from our own doubts and conflicts within.

As we should weep for our own sins, so for the sins of others. As we may see in Jeremiah, where the prophet saith, 'O that my head were a fountain of tears, that I might weep continually for the sins of my people,' Jer. 9:1. And indeed good men are easy to weep, as the heathen man observeth.[1] They are easy to lament, not only for their own sins, but the sins and misery of another.

Our blessed Saviour himself, we never read that he laughed. We have heard that he wept, and for his very enemies, 'O Jerusalem, Jerusalem,' Matt. 23:37. He shed

---

[1] 'Good men are easy to weep, as the heathen man observeth.' Cf. Juvenal, xv. 133.

tears for them that shed his blood. Tears were main evidences of Christ's sweetness of disposition; as that he would become man, and a curse, and die for us, and that he would make so much of little children, and call all to him that were weary and heavy laden, that he never refused any that came to him. He that wept specially for the miseries and afflictions, this shewed his gracious and sweet disposition. And that in heaven, he is so full of sympathies in glory, that when Paul persecuted the church, 'Why dost thou persecute me?' Acts 9:4; so, though he is free from passion in heaven, he is not free from compassion, from sympathy with his church. And so every child of God is ready, not only to grieve for his own sins, and the misery that followeth them, but the sins and miseries of others. 'Mine eyes gush out with rivers of tears,' saith the prophet David, Psa. 119:136, when he saw that men brake the law of God, whom he loved.

A true natural child takes to heart the disgrace of his father. If we be not grieved to see our father disgraced, we are bastards, not sons. They that make sport of sin, what are they? Alas! they have not one spark of the spirit of adoption. They are not children, who rejoice at that at which they should grieve.

So St Paul, 'I have told you often, and now tell you weeping, there be many enemies of the cross of Christ,' Phil. 3:18. When he saw some men preach against, and others enemies of the cross of Christ, whose end is damnation, he telleth them of it weeping.

We have cause, therefore, to mourn for the sins of others, and for the miseries of others, whether we respect God, or the church, or ourselves.

First, the love of God moveth us to weep when we see him dishonoured.

Second, if we love the church, we should mourn for any sins that may prejudice their salvation.

Doth it not pity any[1] man to see an ox go to slaughter? to see a man of parts otherwise, by sinning against conscience, going to slaughter? to see an ordinary swearer, an unclean person, a profane wretch, covering himself with pride as a garment, scorning God, and the world, and all? Can a Christian look upon this, see flesh and blood, like himself, under the gospel, under a cursed condition unavoidable, without serious repentance, and not be affected with it? Can a man see a poor ass fall under a burden, and not help to take it up, and yet see man falling to hell, and not be affected with it? Thus we see we have cause enough of tears. And as there is cause, so we should be sensible. We ought to take to heart the afflictions of Joseph. He is a dead man that hath not sense in this kind. If we go to the body and state, or anything about a man, there is cause of grief. Hath not every member many diseases? and is not our lives a kind of hospital, some sick of one thing, some of another? But as there is cause we should be sensible of it, we are flesh and not stones, therefore it is a sottish opinion, to be stockish and brutish, as if to outface sorrow and grief were a glory.

Use 1. When our Saviour was sent into the world, *Christi dolor, dolor maximus*,[2] there were no patience without sensibleness. Away, then, with that iron, that flinty

---

[1] That is, 'draw pity from any man.'
[2] Latin: 'Christ's grief was grief at its highest pitch.'

philosophy, that thinks it a virtue to be stupid;[1] and as the apostle saith, 'without natural affections,' Rom. 1:31. He counteth it the greatest judgment of God upon the soul, yet they would have it a virtue. Why should I smite them any more? saith God; they have no sense, no feeling, Isa. 1:5.

The proud philosopher thought it was not philosophical to weep, a proud stoical humour,[2] but Christians desire it.

And therefore we ought to labour to be more sensible, that we might make our peace, and reverence the justice of God, and be more sensible of him afterwards. It is most true, that *Sapiens miser, plus miser*; the more wise any man is, the more sensible of misery. And therefore of all men, the best men have most grief, because they have most quick senses. They be not stupified with insensibility and resoluteness, to bear it bravely, as the world; but they apprehend with grief, the cause of grief And as they have a more sanctified judgment than other men, so they have a more wise affection of love, and a quicker life of grace. Where life is, there is sense; and where there is a clear sight or cause of grief, there is most grief. Therefore the best men have most grief, because they be most judicious, most loving.

Then they have most grace to bear it out of all others. Therefore, considering there is cause in ourselves and in others of grief continually, we ought to labour to be sensible of it, else it were no favour to have tears wiped away.

So that there is cause of tears, and tears is a duty of Christians, sensible of the cause both of sin and misery upon one and another.

---

[1] That is, 'insensible.'

[2] One of the commonplaces of *Stoicism*.

Use 2. And as it is an unavoidable grief, *so it is good we should grieve.* We must stoop to God's course, we must bring our hearts to it, and pray (that since our necessities and sins do call for this dispensation, that we must under correction, he will make us sensible of his rod), that he would make good his covenant of grace, 'to take away our stony hearts, and give us hearts of flesh,' Ezek. 11:19, that we may be sensible.

Most of graces are founded upon affection, and all graces are but affections sanctified. What would become of grace, if we had not affections? Therefore, as there is cause of grief, and tears from grief, we ought to grieve. It is a condition, and a duty; a condition following misery, and a duty following our condition.

Take heed of that which hinders sensibleness of troubles and judgment, that is, hardness of heart, forgetfulness, studying to put away sorrow with sin. For we ought to be sensible, and ought to labour to be sensible, to know the meaning of every cross in ourselves and others.

But suppose we have crosses, and we must be sensible of them, then it followeth, 'God will wipe away all tears from our eyes.' Is there nothing for the present, no ground of comfort? Yes. As we ought to be sensible of grief, so we ought to be sensible of matter of joy for the present, specially if we consider the time to come. The life of a Christian is a strange kind of life. He ought to grieve, and he ought to joy. He hath occasion of both, and he ought to entertain both; for that that we ought to aim at specially is joy, and if we grieve, it is that afterwards we might joy. We must be sensible of any affliction, that we might joy afterwards, and we ought to labour for it. For is not the joy of the Lord our strength? Are not we fit to do service, when our spirits are most enlarged? And is it not a credit to religion, when we walk in comfort of the Holy Ghost? Is it not a scandal, when we droop under the cross? We ought to be sensible, yet not so as to forget matter of joy and comfort. And therefore, as we ought to grieve, so we ought, when we have grieved, to keep up the soul, with consideration of joy for the present as much as we can, yea, to pick out matter of comfort from the very cross. That is the heart of a Christian, not only to joy in other matters, but to pick comfort out of grief. God suffers me to fall into this or that condition. It is a fruit of his fatherly love. He might suffer me to run the broad way, to be given up to a reprobate sense and hard heart, but he doth not do so. Pick out matter of comfort from grief.

Then consider the presence of God in it. Indeed, I have matter of grief, but I find God moderating it. It might be far worse, it is his mercy I am not consumed; I find God by it doing me good, I find myself better by it, I cannot well be without it. Who would not labour to be sensible of a cross, when he looketh up to God's cross, and justice, and mercy? He hath rather cause to joy, than to grieve in the very cross itself.

But specially mark what the Holy Ghost saith here. We ought not to be cast down overmuch with any cross, considering God 'will wipe away all tears from our eyes,' that is, all natural tears, and the miseries of this life. There shall be no more misery, no more sickness, no more trouble.

And then all tears that arise from consideration of sin, and misery following sin. Death is the accomplishment of all mortification. It is a comfort we shall not always lead this conflicting life, but the war between the flesh and spirit will be taken up; the sense will be removed. We shall be out of Satan's reach, and the world's reach one day, which is a great comfort to consider. Whatsoever the cause is, the cause shall be removed ere long. If the cause be desertion, for that God leaveth us comfortless, we shall be forever hereafter with the Lord. If the cause be separation from friends, why we shall all meet together ere long, and be forever in heaven. If the cause be our own sins, we shall cease hereafter to offend God, and Christ will be all in all. Now sin is almost all in all. Sin and corruption bear a great sway in us. If the matter of our grief be the sins of others, and the afflictions of others, there is no sin in heaven, 'no unclean thing shall enter there,' Rev. 21:27. The souls of perfect men are there, and all are of one mind. There is no opposition to goodness, there all shall go one way; there, howsoever they cannot agree here, all shall have mutual solace and contentment in one another: they in us and we in them, and that forever. You cannot name them, or imagine a cause of tears, but it shall be removed there. Nay, the more tears we have shed here, the more comfort we shall have. As our troubles are increased here, our consolation shall increase. That we suffer here, if for a good cause, will work our 'eternal and exceeding weight of glory,' 2 Cor. 4:17. We say April showers bring forth May flowers. It is a common speech, from experience of common life. It is true in religion. The more tears we shed in the April of our lives, the more sweet comfort we shall have hereafter, If no tears are to be shed here, no flowers are to be gathered there. And, therefore, besides deliverance from trouble, here is comfort, God will take away all cause of grief, and all kinds of grief whatsoever.

And therefore thus think of it.

The next thing to be considered is the order. First, we must shed tears, and then they must be wiped away. After a storm, a calm; after sowing in tears, comes reaping in joy. What is the reason of that order?

Reason 1. The reason is *our own necessity*. We are in such a frame and condition since the fall, that we cannot be put into a good frame of grace without much pain. The truths of God must cross us, and afflictions must join with them. For the sins contracted by pleasure, must be dissolved by pain. Repentance must cost us tears. We may thank ourselves if we have brought ourselves to a sinful course. For the necessity of this order, a diseased person must not be cured till he feel some smart of the wounds.

Reason 2. Again, consider it is *for our increase of comfort afterwards*, that God will have us shed tears; and then to have our tears wiped away, because we be more sensible of joy and comfort after sorrow. We cannot be sensible of the joys of heaven, unless we feel the contrary here. And therefore of all men, heaven will be the most heaven to them that have had their portion of crosses and afflictions here. First, therefore, shed tears, and then they must be wiped away, because joy is most sensible. As it is with the wickedest of all men, they be most miserable that have been happiest, because their soul is enlarged by their happiness, to apprehend sorrow more quickly and sensibly. So they that have been most miserable here, shall have most joy hereafter.

Use 1. Now for use. Here is not only the mercies of God in Christ, but the tender mercy; that whereas our life is full of tears, which we have brought upon ourselves, yet God stoops so low as to wipe our eyes, like a father or mother.

His mercy is a sweet and tender mercy. And, as the psalmist saith, when we are sick 'he maketh our beds in our sickness,' Psa. 41:3. Christ will come and serve them that watch and serve him; nay, he will attend them, and 'sup with them,' Rev. 3:20. He is not only mercy and goodness, but there be in him bowels of mercy. He not only giveth matter of joy and comfort, but he will do like a tender-hearted mother, wiping away all tears from our eyes. We cannot apprehend the bowels in God's love, the pity and mercy of God towards them that be his, and afflicted in the world, specially in a good cause. Though they be never so many, if they be penitent tears, he will wipe them all away.

And whereas we must shed tears here, that we may be comforted hereafter, take heed that we do not in this life judge by sight, but by faith. 'If we live by sight, we are of all men most wretched,' 1 Cor. 15:19. In the world the children of God are most miserable, and of the children of God, the best saints. Who hath more cause of tears than the best saints? It is but seed-time here. While seed-time continues, there be tears. The husbandman, while it is seed-time, cannot do his office but with trouble. The minister cannot do his office, but he is forced to take to heart the sins of the times, to see his work go backward. Governors of families and such, they carry their seed weeping. Yea, the best men cannot do good sometimes, but they do it with trouble in themselves, and with conflict of corruptions. There is no good sown here, but it is sown in tears; yet take no scandal at this, 'God will wipe away all tears.'

The Head of the church, our blessed Saviour, and all his gracious apostles, what a life did they live! The glorious martyrs that sealed the truth with their blood! And therefore, as the apostle saith, 'If our happiness were here only, we were of all men most miserable,' 1 Cor. 15:19. If we judge by sight, we shall condemn the generation of the righteous. We live by sight, when we see any cast down with sight of sin, sense of temptation, distress of conscience, [and] we think him forlorn. Oh, take heed of that! For those that shed tears here, God will wipe them all away. 'Woe to them that laugh now, for they shall mourn hereafter,' Luke 6:25. Though we weep here, yet matter of joy enough shall spring up hereafter. 'Afflictions will yield a quiet fruit of righteousness to them that are exercised thereby,' Heb. 12:11. We may not see their fruits presently, but afterwards. And therefore be not discouraged for anything we can suffer here, or for the church, if we see her under pressure. As darkness is sown for the wicked, the foundation of their eternal torment is laid in their joy; so the ground and foundation of all a godly man's joy is laid in tears. 'Blessed are they that mourn, for they shall be comforted,' Matt. 5:4. Yet for the present there is more matter of joy than grief, if we look with both eyes; as we ought to have double eyes, one to be sensible of our grief, as we must be, the other of our comfort, that we may not be surprised with grief. There is a sorrow to death, an overmuch sorrow. It is unthankfulness to God to forget our comforts, as it is stupidity to forget our sorrow. Take us at the worst, have not we more cause of joy than sorrow? Mark Rom. 5:1, *seq.*: 'Being justified by faith, we have peace with God, and rejoice under hope of glory.' Nay, afterwards, saith he, 'we rejoice in tribulations.' And why? upon what ground? 'Knowing that tribulations bring experience, and experience hope, and hope maketh not ashamed.' Now we rejoice in God reconciled in Christ.

So that as we ought to look with one eye upon the grief, that we may have ground to exercise grace, which we are not capable of without sensibleness, so we must look to grounds of joy. Our life is woven of matter of sorrow and joy; and as it is woven of both, affections should be sensible of both, that they may be more apprehensive of the grounds of comforts.

When the day of persecution approacheth, this will make us comfortable, for our life is a valley of tears; and shall not we go through this valley of tears, to this mount where all tears shall be wiped away from all eyes? When we be dejected with the loss of any friend, they say as Christ said to the women, 'Weep not for me,' Luke 23:28. They be happy, 'and all tears are wiped away from their eyes': And therefore as it is matter of comfort while we live, so ground of comfort when we die. For there is occasion of sorrow in death, parting with friends and comforts of this world. Then tears are shed in more abundance, and then we bethink ourselves of former sins, and there is renewing of repentance more than at other times; yet then are we near the time of joy, and nearest the accomplishment of the promise that 'all tears shall be wiped away.'

And so you have the whole state of a Christian life, an afflicted condition. Aye, but it is a comfortable condition. The more afflictions here, the more comfort here, but specially hereafter. The life of a carnal man is all in misery. If he falls to joy, he is all joy; if to sorrow, he is all sorrow. He hath nothing to support him. He is like a Nabal, he sinketh like a piece of lead to the bottom of the sea, 1 Sam. 25:37, 38; like Ahithophel, down he goeth, 2 Sam. 17:23. When he is upon the merry pin, he is nothing but joy. But a Christian's state and disposition are both mixed. He hath ground of sorrow for his own sins, and for the sins and miseries of the times. So he hath matter of comfort for the present, in the favour of God, in the pardoning of sins, in the presence of God, in delivering him from trouble. He hath special ground of joy in hope of glory in time to come. Therefore, as we have a mixed state, labour for a mixed disposition, and labour to be in a joyful frame, so to grieve, as out of it to raise matter of joy. And when we would joy, grieve before, for joy is sown in grief. The best method of joy is for to take away all that disturbeth our joy. Search the bottom of the heart! see what sin is unconfessed, unrepented of! Spread it before God, desire God to pardon it, to seal the pardon! When our souls are searched to the bottom, then out of that sorrow springeth joy; and out of these sighs and groans that cannot be expressed, cometh joy unspeakable and full of glory. If a man will be joyful, let him labour to weep first, that the matter that interrupteth his joy may be taken away. Those that will be joyful, and not search to the bottom, must needs with shame be brought back to sorrow. When we will joy to purpose, let us judge ourselves, that we may not be judged of the Lord; mourn for our sins, and then lay hold upon the promise, that 'all they that mourn for sin shall be comforted,' Matt. 5:4. And blessed are they that shed tears here, for all tears shall be wiped away.

We are subject to wrong ourselves, both good and bad: for the good think, if they be in misery, they shall be ever so; the bad, if they be in prosperity, they shall always be so, and they bless themselves in it. Now the joy of the hypocrites is as the 'crackling of thorns,' Eccles. 7:6, and the grief of the godly is but short. And therefore let not the wicked fool themselves with groundless hopes, nor the godly vex themselves with needless fears; but put off conceitedness of the long continuance of troubles. Time is but short, and ere long God 'will wipe away all tears from our eyes.' No mists, no clouds, shall be extended to heaven. The state in heaven shall be like the state of heaven, and there is no cloud there, but all pure, all serene. Therefore in Christianity consider not their beginning but their ends. 'Mark the end of the upright, for the end of the upright is peace,' Psa. 37:37. Ways have their commendation from the term in which they end. 'If by any means I may attain the resurrection of the dead,' saith Paul, Phil. 3:11. Through thick and thin, fair and foul, rugged winds, dry or bloody death; if by any means I may come to the resurrection of the dead, the first degree of glory, all is well. It is a good way that ends well. *Non qua, sed quo.* Consider not what way he brings us to heaven, but whither he brings us. If he bring us to heaven through a valley of tears, it is no matter; for in heaven 'all tears shall be wiped from our eyes.' And therefore Christianity is called wisdom. 'And this wisdom is justified of her children,' Matt. 11:19. What is the chiefest point of wisdom? To look home to the end, and to direct all means to that end. He is wise that is wise for eternity. The wicked will have their payment here. 'But woe to them that laugh, for they shall mourn,' saith Christ, Luke 6:25. They will not stay for ground of joy hereafter, but will have present payment. But though the ways of Christians be foul, and wet with tears, yet blessed are they; for God 'will wipe away all tears from their eyes.' 'Comfort one another with these words,' 1 Thess. 4:18.

Sermon 6

And he shall swallow up death in victory; and God will wipe away tears from all faces; that the rebukes of his people may be taken away from off the earth: for the Lord hath spoken it.

– Isaiah 25:8

YOU have heard heretofore of a *feast* provided for God's people, the *founder* of it being God himself, who only can indeed comfort (that which is specially to be comforted) the soul and the conscience, he being above the conscience. The *place* where the feast is kept is 'mount Zion,' the church of God. The delicacies are described by 'fat things, wine refined on the lees,' etc. The best of the best that can be thought of, which is Christ with all his benefits; who is bread indeed, and drink indeed, that cherisheth and nourisheth the soul to life everlasting. And because there should be nothing to disturb the solemnity of the feast, he promises to 'destroy the face of covering,' 'to take away the veil spread over all nations,' the veil of ignorance and infidelity, to shine upon the soul, and fill it full of knowledge and heavenly comfort. And because there can be no comfort where death is feared, being the greatest enemy in this life, therefore he will 'swallow up death in victory,' and all that makes way for death, or attends death. And when this is taken away,

[95]

all the attendants vanish with it, 'God will wipe away all tears from all faces.' Because the best things have not the best entertainment in the world, nor the best persons, God promiseth that the rebukes of his people shall be taken away from off the earth; what they are they shall be known to be. These be very great matters, and therefore there is a great confirmation, they have a seal, and what is that? 'The Lord hath spoken it.'

The last day I shewed that God's children shall shed tears, and that they have cause to do it. I will now enlarge it a little.

It is the condition of men since the fall. In paradise before there was no cause of tears, nothing was out of joint, all in frame. There was no sin, therefore no sorrow, therefore no apprehension of sorrow. And so in heaven there shall be no tears, because no cause of it; they shall be as far from heaven as the cause. This life is a valley of tears, a life of misery, and therefore we shed tears here. And we want no cause of it as long as sin is in the world, and sorrow, and misery that followeth sin; our own sins and the sins of others, our own miseries and the miseries of others. And surely a child of God finds this the greatest cause of mourning in this world, that he hath a principle in him always molesting him in the service of God. He cannot serve God with that cheerfulness. His unfeelingness, that he cannot be so sensible of God, dishonoured by himself and others, is his burden. He is grieved that he cannot grieve enough. He can find tears for other things, matter of this enough, as the heathen man could say.[1] A man loseth his estate, and hath tears for them;

---

[1] 'He can find tears,' etc. Cf. Seneca, *de Consolatione ad Polybium*, 4, § 2.

but forceth tears for other things which are the true ground of grief. A child of God hath a remainder of corruptions, which puts him on to offend against God, and hinders him in his service, in the liberty and cheerfulness of it. And this he complains of with Paul and others, 'Miserable man that I am,' not for his affliction, though that was much, but 'who shall deliver me from this body of death?' Rom. 7:24.

Case 1. I will here add a case. *Some say they cannot weep, but they can grieve; whether then is it necessary or no to weep?* Tears are taken for the spring of tears; grief, all grief, shall be taken away. Tears are but the messengers of grief; and oftentimes the deepest apprehension, that takes things deeply, cannot express it in tears. In some the passages fetching the conceit to the heart are made more tender that they can weep. Now, the grief of a Christian is a judicial[1] grief; a rational grief, not only sensible tears must have sensible grief, but a Christian's grief is a sensible, judicial grief. He hath a right judgment of things that cause sorrow, willeth it, and tears are only an expression of it.

But how shall I know whether grief be right or no? There be tears God hath no bottle for. 'Thou puttest my tears into thy bottle,' Psa. 56:8. He makes much of them. They be *vinum angelicum*,[2] as he saith. God is an angel to his people, to wipe away their tears. But some tears God hath no bottle for, hypocritical tears, Delilah's tears, tears of revenge and anger, Esau's tears. And therefore the true tears that God will wipe away, are such as first of all follow our condition

[1] That is, 'judicious.'
[2] Latin: 'the wine of angels.'

here, our misery. God will wipe them away. If we speak of tears from a judicial ground,

1. The spring of true tears is *the love of God, and of Christ, and of his church, and the love of the state of Christianity.* Tears spring from love, these tears specially.

Oh! a Christian takes to heart that God should be so ill used in the world; that Christ, the Saviour of the world, should find such entertainment, that he should have anything in him that should offend such a Saviour! This unkindness stingeth him to the heart. He takes it grievously that God should be abused. *Lætitia habet suas lachrymas*,[1] there is not only grief that is the immediate cause of tears, but another cause beforehand; that is, love. Joy likewise hath its tears, though they be not here meant specially.

2. Again, tears are good and sound when we weep for our own sins as well as the sins and miseries of others. And I will add more, we must weep for the sins of others as well as for our own. For it is a greater sign of the truth of grace to take to heart the sins of others more than our own. You will say this is a kind of paradox, for often a man may take to heart his own sins as matter of terror of conscience; not his sins, as contrary to God, having antipathy to him, being opposite to the state of the soul, not as sin is properly sin, but to be grieved and vexed for sin as it hath vexation and terror of conscience. When a man can take to heart the sins of another, and that truly as it is an offence of his good God, and a crucifying again of his sweet Saviour, these be true tears indeed. It is more sign of grace than to weep for a man's own sins.

[1] Latin: 'Joy has its own tears.'

Some are taken up with terrors of conscience, that let their children, family, and friends alone. Their heart is eaten up with self-love, and they be near eaten up with their own terrors of conscience. But here is true grief and an hatred of sin in a right respect, when it exerciseth itself upon others as well as upon ourselves.

3. Again, tears arise from the right spring, from true grief, *when we can weep in secret*. Oh! saith Jeremiah, if you do so and so, 'My soul shall weep in secret for your pride,' Jer. 13:17. Here was a good soul indeed. Many will have tears of comfort in public, etc. Aye, but when they can weep in secret for their own sins and the sins of others, it is an evidence of a right spring of grief.

4. Again, when tears tend *to reformation of what they grieve for*; for else they be *steriles lachrymæ*, barren tears. Do they tend to reform what we weep for? Do they tend to action? Affections are then good when they carry to action; as grief, love, joy, they are all for action. When we weep and grieve, and reform withal, it is a good sign. I will name no more. You see then that grief is sound when it springeth from the love of God, and is for the sins of others as well as our own, and our own as well as others; when it stirs up to reformation; when it is in secret; and therefore let us examine our grief by these and the like evidences. It will be a good character of a gracious soul. Then God will carry himself as a sweet nurse, or loving mother to her child, that sheddeth tears. God will 'wipe away all these tears.' Oh! the transcending love of God! His love is a tender love. The love of a mother, the love of a nurse! It is not love, but the bowels of love, the bowels of mercy and compassion. How low doth he stoop to wipe away the tears of his children! 'God will wipe away all tears.'

I will propound one question more, and then proceed. But we are bid to rejoice always. Why then is it required that we weep and mourn? Can two contraries stand together?

Case 2. I answer, very well. For we may grieve, as we have matter of grief, and are in a condition of grief; and we may rejoice, and ought to rejoice, as we look to the promise that God 'will wipe away all tears.' When we think of the present cause, we cannot but grieve; but when we look beyond all troubles, we cannot but joy; it hath influence of joy into our heart. Nay, for the present we may joy and grieve, without looking to eternity sometimes. If we consider that we have offended God, done that that grieveth his Spirit, that is matter of grief. But when we consider we have Christ at his right hand, that speaketh peace for us, and makes our peace by virtue of his mediation, that giveth comfort. So that we have cause of joy, and cause of grief, about the same things at the same time.

We are never in such a state of grief here, but if we look about us, look forward, look upward ...[1] A Christian, that is, a good Christian, is a person that hath many things to look after, that he may manage his estate of Christianity wisely. He is to look to himself and his sins, to the mercies of God in Christ, to the constancy of it, that it is answerable to the fruit of it in peace and joy here, and happiness hereafter, which are constant too. His grace, as himself, is constant, the fruits of it constant. Therefore 'rejoice evermore.' And, saith the apostle, 'I know what I say, I am well advised, "evermore rejoice,"' Phil. 4:4. So that the life of a Christian is a mixed life, nay, the ground of our joy is our sorrow and grief, and

---

[1] This sentence is left thus unfinished.

joy is sown in grief. If we will rejoice indeed, let us mourn indeed. True joy ariseth and springs out of sorrow.

I proceed to the next. 'And the rebukes of his people shall be taken away from off the face of the earth.' Another benefit that makes the feast sweet and comfortable is this: 'He will take away the rebukes of his people.' And here is the same method to be used, *that God's children, his church, and people, are under rebukes, and under reproach.*

We need not stand to prove the truth of it. It is true, *first, the head of the church, and the church itself, and every particular member, they go under rebukes.* For the head of the church, we should spend the time to no purpose to prove it. What was Christ's life? It was under a veil. He appeared not to be what he was. You know he was esteemed the chief of devils, an enemy to his prince, to Caesar. I will not spend time in clear truths.

For the church itself, you see in the book of Esther, 3:8, 'There is a strange people that acknowledge no law, they be against the laws of the prince.' They pass under the imputation of rebels. The poor church, that had thoughts of peace, the meek church of God, they counted as enemies of the state, as Christ, the head, was. And so the church in Babylon, under what rebukes was it? They reproached them, 'By the waters of Babylon we sat down and wept, when they said, Sing us one of the songs of Zion,' Psa. 137:1. The church sitteth by the waters of Babylon all this life. The world is a kind of Babylon to God's people, and then sing us one of your songs. Where is now your God? say the hearts of wretched people, when they saw the people of God in disgrace. Tully[1] could say of the nation of the Jews, 'It

---

[1] That is, Cicero.

THE GLORIOUS FEAST OF THE GOSPEL

sheweth how God regardeth it; it hath been so often over-come.'[1] Thus the heathen man could scorn the state of God's people. You see how the psalmist complains in the name of particular Christians, 'Where is his God? he trusted in him, let him save him,' Psa. 22:8. Oh, this was daggers to David's heart. 'It pierced to my heart when they said, Where is thy God?' Psa. 42:10. To touch a Christian in his God, as if God had no care of him, it is more than his own grief and affliction. So when a child of God is rebuked and affronted, when religion must suffer by it, so that the head of the church, the members of the church, are under rebukes, as it may be proved, if I carry you through all stories.

At this day, the church of the Jews, you see what it is come to: the nation of the Jews, under what reproach it is. And surely this prophecy aimeth partly at the conversion of the Jews. It shall be accomplished at the resurrection, when all tears shall be perfectly wiped away. But it hath relation to the conversion of the Jews. In what state are they now? Are they not a word of reproach? Moses' speech is verified of them, 'They shall be a hissing to all nations,' 2 Chron. 29:8. And is not it a proverb, Hated as a Jew?

Reason. But what is the reason of it? Not to stand long upon the point, you know there be two seeds in the world, the seed of the serpent and the seed of the woman; and the enmity between them is the true ground, and the antipathy in the hearts of carnal men to goodness. There is a light shineth in the life of them that be good, and them that be ill hate the light, as discovering themselves to themselves, and to the world, not to be that they seem to be. There is

[1] Cicero, *Oratio Pro Flacco*, c. 28. This is one of only two notices of the Jews that are found in the voluminous works of Cicero.

a saltness in the truth. It is savoury, but it is tart, whether in the word preached, or howsoever truth layeth open what is cross to corruption. And hereupon pride and self-love in carnal men studieth how to overcast all they can the names of those that be better than themselves with a cloud of disgrace. It is the property of vile men to make all others vile, that they may be alike. Men cannot abide distinctions of one from another. The Scripture distinguisheth the 'righteous man, more excellent than his neighbour,' Prov. 12:26; but they will not have that. The hatred of distinction is the cause they make all as bad as they can. And hereupon it is that good things were never clothed in the right habit, nor ill things neither, but do pass under a veil. Take away the true garment of grace and holiness and goodness, and put a false veil upon it, it passeth not under that that it is in this world, because wicked men will not suffer it, but will raise up the credit of other things, of empty learning, or empty things, or vain courses, and cry up the credit of worldly things, that they may seem to be wise, and not fools, that are carried to those things. The best things had never the happiness to pass under their own names; but they had other coverings. Truth goeth always with a torn and scratched face; it is a stranger in the world, and hath strange entertainment.

Use 1. If this be so, we ought to take heed of laying a scandal or reproach upon religion. Salvian complains in his time that wickedness had gotten that head, that those that were good and honourable, *mali esse volunt, ne a malis abhorreantur,*[1] they that were good studied to be vile, that

---

[1] 'Salvian complains in his time,' etc. The thought is found in Salvianus de Gubernat. Dei., lib. 4, p. 74 (edition 1669).

they might not be vilified of others. 'Oh,' saith he, 'how much is Christ beholden to the world, that those that own him, and own goodness, and own his cause, should be therefore base, because they be his friends.' Take heed of taking scandals.

Use 2. We had need be wise, that we be not taken in this snare of Satan, *to mistake error for truth, and good for evil.* Satan and his agents make things pass under contrary representations. Superstition goeth for religion, and religion for superstition, schism, and heresy. It hath always been so. Therefore seek wisdom to discern aright. The devil hath two properties, he is a liar and a murderer; the one makes way for the other, for he could not murder unless he did lie. The devil himself will not be an open murderer if he can help it. The fraudulent persecution is worse than the violent. If he can bring to hell by fraud and lying, he will never do it by violence. He is a liar, that he may be a murderer; for when he can raise an imputation upon the church and children of God, that they be rebels, enemies of state, then he may *cum privilegio*[1] be a murderer. When he hath tainted God's people in the conceit of the world, then they find that entertainment not which they deserve, but which they be apprehended to deserve, when the conceit of other men towards them is poisoned. 'Oh, this sect is spoken against everywhere,' say they to Paul, Acts 28:22. Therefore we had need be wise; for if the instruments of Satan, led with his spirit, had not hoped that slanders should take, they would never have been so skilful in that trade. But they know they shall find some shallow fools

[1] Latin: 'with due licence.'

that will believe them, without searching into the depths
of them, and take up persons and things under prejudice.
It is enough for them that this is said of them. They have
neither wit nor judgment, nor so much patience, from
following their lusts, as to examine them; and that makes
them so mad as they are. *Calumniare audacter, aliquid
hærebit*, slander stoutly, something will stick, they are sure
of it. That which hath raised and ruined many a man, is that
of Haman's casting of jealousy upon those that are better
than themselves. That was Haman's trick, and so will be the
practice of the wicked, as it hath been from the beginning,
so to the end of the world. 'Thou art not Caesar's friend,' say
they, and it is enough to Pilate, John 19:12. Thus it has been,
and will be to the end of the world. Therefore we had need
to be wise, that we be not misled. Men will never leave to
speak ill till they have learned to speak better, till the Spirit
of God hath taught them.

Now, it is said that Christ will take away the rebukes of
his people. That is the promise. As they are, they shall be
known to be. He will set all in joint again. Harmony is a
sweet thing, and order is a sweet thing. Time will come
when things that are now out of order to appearance, shall
be all set in their due order again. Those that are basest shall
be lowest, and those that be excellent shall be highest. This
is a-working and framing now. In this confusion we must
look to the catastrophe, the conclusion of all. He will 'take
away the rebukes of all.' God is the father of truth, and truth
is the daughter of time. Time will bring forth truth at last.
And those that be honourable indeed shall be honourable.
It is as true as God is just; for goodness and holiness are
beams of God; and will he suffer it always to pass under a

false veil? There is not an attribute of God but shall shine forth gloriously, even all his excellency and dignity. There is nothing shall be above him and his excellency. No; though he seems for a while not to rule in the world, or have power, but suffers them to go away with it that are his enemies, he is working another thing by suffering them, he is working the glory of his children, and confusion of his enemies. There is nothing in God but shall gloriously shine, and nothing in his children, no beams of God, but shall gloriously shine, to the confusion of the world. They that are good shall be known to be good, God will bring their righteousness to light. The witnesses that vexed the world, and had base entertainment, they were slain and disgraced, but they rose again, and were carried to heaven, Rev. 11:12, *seq.*, as Elijah. So there will be a resurrection of name, a resurrection of reputation. That that is good shall be good, and that that is bad shall be bad. It shall be known to be as it is. This is for comfort.

Use 1. You hear, therefore, what course to take under disgrace. What shall we do when the church passeth under disgrace, as it is now? A protestant is worse than a Turk or a Jew amongst the railing papists. Among ourselves we see under what reputation the best things go. It is too well known to speak of. And the scandal taken from hence doth extremely harden. It keeps men from religion, it draweth many from religion that have entered into it, because they have not learned so much self-denial as to venture upon disgrace. And surely where no self-denial is, there is no religion. Christ knew what doctrine he taught when he taught self-denial in this respect.

What shall we do, therefore?

1. Labour first of all for *innocency*, that if men will reproach, they may reproach without a cause.

2. Then labour for a *spirit of patience* to serve Christ with. 'Great is your reward when men speak evil of you,' Matt. 5:12, for a good cause. It is the portion of a Christian in this life to do well and suffer ill. Of all, certainly they are best, that, out of love to goodness, are carried to goodness, without looking to rewards or disgrace; that follow with a single eye. Labour, therefore, for patience, and not only so, but,

3. For *courage*. For the moon goeth its course, and lets the dog bark. We have a course to run, let us keep our course constantly; pass through good reports and bad reports; be at a point what the world thinks. We seek applause at another theatre than the world.

4. Again, then, labour for *sincerity under rebukes*, that we have a good aim, such an aim as Paul had, 'If I be mad and out of my wits,' 2 Cor. 5:13, 14. He being earnest for his master, Christ, they count him out of his wits. If I be out of my wits it is for Christ. 'If I be sober, it is for you, the love of Christ constraineth me to be so,' 2 Cor. 5:14. Get the love of Christ, and that will make a man care for nothing. If I go beyond myself, it is to God. As David said, when he was mocked by Michal, 'It is to the Lord,' when he danced before the ark, 2 Sam. 6:20, 21. *Bonus ludus*, a good dance, where Michal scoffeth, and David danceth. Where gracious men magnify God, and have Michals to scoff at them, it is *bonus ludus*. God will look upon them, for it is to the Lord. Labour that our aims be good, and it is no matter what the world judgeth of them.

5. And when all will not do, *commend our credits to God by prayer*. As we commend our souls and conditions, so our reputations, that he would take care of them, that he would bring our righteousness to light, that it should shine out as the noonday. So David doth, he complains to God; and commendeth all to him, prayeth him to take part against his enemies, to right his cause. And when we have done that, we have done our duty. Yet withal hope for better things, be content to pass under the world as unknown men, and to be inwardly worthy, and pass as unknown men. Rich men, if truly rich, they will applaud themselves in their bosoms, though the world disgrace them, yet at home I am thus furnished. And so a Christian that knoweth his worth, that he is a child of God, heir of heaven, that he is attended upon by angels, that he is a jewel to God in his esteem, he thinks this to be absolutely the best thing in the world. He knoweth the worth of a Christian, and his own worth as being a Christian. He applauseth[1] and comforteth himself, in that he knoweth he hath a hidden life, a state of glory hidden in Christ. Now it is covered with disgrace and disrespect in the world, scorned and reproached, but what is that to him? It is an hidden life, and for the present he knoweth his own excellency, and, therefore, can pass through good report and bad report. 'I care not for man's day,' saith Paul, 'there is another day to which I must stand,' 1 Cor. 4:3.

And thus if we do, as Peter saith, 'There is a spirit of glory shall rest upon us,' 1 Pet. 4:14. The ground we have of comfort under rebuke and disgrace, there is a spirit of glory. What is that? A large spirit enlarging our hearts with inward comfort, inward joy, inward love of God. 'A spirit

[1] That is, 'applaudeth.'

of glory shall rest upon you,' and shall continue with you as long as disgrace shall continue. He opposeth this to all disgrace he meeteth with in the world.

God putteth sometimes a glory and excellency upon his children under disgrace and ill usage in the world, that he will daunt the world, as Stephen's face did shine as the face of an angel, which came from a spirit of glory that rested upon him, and expressed himself to be the servant of God. He that takes away from our good report, if we be good, he addeth to our reward. Our Saviour Christ saith as much, 'Blessed are you when you be ill spoken of, for great is your reward'; Matt. 5:11, 12.

Sermon 7

And the rebukes of his people shall he take away from all the earth: for the Lord hath spoken it.

– Isaiah 25:8

USE 3. This is a great promise, *and I pray you be comforted with it.* For of all grief that God's people suffer in the world, there is none greater than reproach, disgrace, and contumely. *Movemur contumeliis plus quam injuriis*, we are more moved with reproaches than injuries. Injuries come from several causes, but disgrace from abundance of slighting. No man but thinks himself worthy of respect from some or other. Now, slanders come from abundance of malice, or else abundance of contempt; and therefore nothing sticks so much as reproaches, specially by reason of opinion and fancy, that raiseth them over high.

Our Saviour, Christ, 'endured the cross and despised the shame,' Heb. 12:2. That shame that vain people cast upon religion and the best things, they despise that and make that a matter of patience. They knew the cross would not be shaken off, persecution and troubles must be endured, and therefore they 'endured the cross, and despised the shame.' Now, to bear crosses, take the counsel of the holy apostles, look up to him, consider Christ; and whatsoever disgrace in words or carriage we shall endure, we are sure, though we shall never know it till we feel it by experience, 'the spirit of glory shall rest upon us,' and rebuke shall be taken away.

Ere long there will be no glory in heaven and earth but the glory of Christ and of his spouse, for all the rest shall be in their own place, as it was said of Judas, that 'he went to his place,' Acts 1:25. Their proper place is not to domineer, but to be in hell, and ere long they shall be there. Heaven is the proper element of the saints; that is the place of Christ, the head, and where should the body be but with the head? where the spouse but with the husband? I say this shall come to pass, that all the wicked shall be in their place, and all the godly in theirs with Christ, and then shall the rebukes of God's people be taken away. A great matter, and therefore it is sealed with a great confirmation, 'The Lord Jehovah hath spoken it.' Therefore it must and will be so. 'The mouth of the Lord hath spoken it.' This is not in vain added, for the Lord knoweth well enough we need it to believe so great things, that there is such a feast provided, and that there is such a victory over death, our last enemy, and that there will be such glory, that all the glory shall be Christ's and his spouse's, that the wicked that are now so insolent shall be cast into their proper place with the devil, by whose spirit they are led. They be great matters, and there is great disproportion between the present condition and that condition in heaven; and infidelity being in the soul, it is hard to fasten such things on the soul, that so great things should be done. But they are no greater than God hath said, and he is able to make good his word. 'The Lord hath said it,' and when God hath said it, heaven and earth cannot unsay it. When heaven hath concluded it, earth and hell cannot disannul it. 'The mouth of the Lord hath spoken it'; that is, truth itself hath spoken it that cannot lie. A man may lie and be a man, and an honest man too. He may sometimes speak an untruth; it taketh not away his nature. But God, who is pure truth, unchangeable truth, truth itself, cannot lie.

When we hear of great matters, as matters of Christianity be great matters, they be as large as the capacity of the soul, and larger too, and yet the soul is large in the understanding and affection too; when we hear of such large matters, we need a great faith to believe them. Great faith needeth great grounds, and therefore it is good to have all the helps we can. When we hear of great things promised, great deliverances, great glory, to strengthen our faith, remember God hath spoken them. He knoweth our weakness, our infirmity, and therefore helps us with this prop, 'The mouth of the Lord hath spoken it.' Let us therefore remember those great things are promised in the word of God, in the word of Jehovah, that can make them all good, that gives a being to all his promises. He is being itself, and gives being to whatsoever he saith. He is able to do it. Set God and his power against all opposition whatsoever from the creature, and all doubts that may arise from our own unbelieving hearts, 'The mouth of the Lord hath spoken it.'

Question. But ye will say, the prophet Isaiah saith it, whose words they were.

Answer. I answer, Isaiah was the penman, God the mouth. The head dictateth, the hand writeth. Christ the head dictates, and his servant writeth. So that holy men write as they were inspired by the Holy Ghost, a better spirit than their own. 'Why do ye look on me?' saith Isaiah. Think not it is I that say it; I am but a man like yourselves; but 'the mouth of the Lord hath spoken it.'

We should not regard men, nor the ministry of men, but consider who speaks by men, who sendeth them, with what commission do they come. Ambassadors are not regarded for themselves, but for them that send them. And therefore Cornelius said well, 'We are here in the presence of God to hear what thou wilt speak in the name of God,' Acts 10:33. And so people should come with that reverent expression, We are come in the presence of God the Father, Son, and Holy Ghost, in the presence of the blessed angels, to hear what thou shalt say in the name of God, by the Spirit of God. We are not to deal with men, but with God. And therefore he saith, 'The mouth of the Lord hath spoken it.'

Question 2. Hence may this question be easily answered, Whence hath the Scripture authority?

Answer. Why, from itself. It is the word; it carrieth its own letters testimonial with it. Shall God borrow authority from men? No; the authority the word hath is from itself. It hath a supreme authority from itself. And we may answer that question about the judge of all controversies, What is the supreme Judge? The word, the Spirit of God in the Scriptures. And who is above God? It is a shameless, ridiculous impudency of men that will take upon them to be judges of Scripture, as if man would get upon the throne, and as a judge there judge. The Scriptures must judge all ere long, yea, that great antichrist. Now an ignorant man, a simple man, that perhaps never read Scriptures, must judge of all controversies, yea, that that is judge of all and of himself, the word, which is from the very mouth of God.

Quest. 3. You will ask me, How shall I know it is the word of God if the church tells us not?

Ans. A carrier sheweth us these be letters from such a man, but when we open the letter, and see the hand and seal, we know them to be his. The church knows the word, and explaineth it; and when we see and feel the efficacy of the word in itself, then we believe it to be the word, for there is that in the word that sheweth it to be the word:

1. The *majesty* that is in it.

2. The matter that is *mysterious*, forgiveness of sins through a mystery, victory over death, life everlasting in the world to come, great matters, 'which eye hath not seen, nor ear heard, nor entered into the heart of man,' 1 Cor. 2:9. If it had not been revealed, it could not have entered into the heart of angels, it containeth such glorious, transcending mysteries. And then again,

3. The word to all them that belong to God *hath the Spirit of God*, by which it passeth, rightly accompanying it, witnessing to the soul of man that it is so; and,

4. *By a divine efficacy* it is mighty in operation. What doth it in the heart? (1.) It warmeth the heart upon the hearing, and speaking, and discoursing of it, as when the disciples went to Emmaus, Luke 24:32. (2.) It hath a heat of Spirit going with it to affect the heart with heavenly joy and delight; it hath power going with it by the Spirit to raise joy unspeakable and glorious; it hath a power to pacify the soul amidst all troubles. When nothing will still the soul, the Spirit of God in the word will do it by its divine power. (3.) Yea, it will change a man from a beastly or devilish temper to a higher and happier estate, as you have it, Isaiah 11:6-9. It makes lions lambs, leopards kids.

And what is the ground of all? In that very place 'the earth shall be full of the knowledge of the Lord.' The knowledge of God reconciled is such a powerful knowledge that it hath a transforming virtue to alter men's dispositions. What was Paul before conversion? and Zaccheus? Therefore, it is the word, because it hath divine operation to heat the soul, and raise the soul, and change the soul, and (4.) cast down the soul, as low in a manner as hell, in sense of its own misery. It will make a Felix to tremble, a man that it doth not effectually work upon. The truths of it are so moving that it will make a carnal man to quake. When Paul spake of judgment to come, of giving account of all that is done in the flesh, when a possibility of it was apprehended, it made Felix to quake. It makes mountains level, and it fills up the valleys. The word can raise up the soul; when man is as low as hell, and looketh for nothing but damnation, the Spirit with the word will fetch him from thence; as the jailor, Acts 16:31, there was little between him and hell, 'What shall I do to be saved? Why, believe in the Lord Jesus.' And with these words there went out an efficacy. He believed, and he afterward was full of joy.

The first gospel ever preached in pardon was by God himself. Never was any creature so near damnation as our first father Adam, cast from the greatest happiness, *miserrimum est fuisse felicem*;[1] for he that enjoyed before communion with God and his angels, having sinned, and having conscience of his sin, considering his great parts, and apprehension of the state he had been in, this must needs affect him deeply; and being in this condition, the

---

[1] Latin: 'It is the most wretched condition to have been once blessed.'

promise of the 'seed of the woman to break the serpent's head,' revived him.

There is a strange efficacy in the gospel. The Roman empire was the greatest enemy that the church ever had. The ten persecutions you see what they were;[1] and yet notwithstanding the word grew upon them and never rested, the spreading of the gospel, and the Spirit with it, till the cross got above the crown, as it did in the time of Constantine, and so it continueth.

5. And must not this be a divine word which hath this efficacy, to revive, comfort, change, cast down, raise up again; *search secrets, search the heart to the bottom*? A poor idiot[2] that comes to hear the word of God, when he hears the secrets of his heart laid open by the word, he concludes certainly, 'God is in you, and you are God's ministers,' 1 Cor. 14:25. The word 'divideth between the marrow and the bone,' Heb. 4:12; it arraigneth the heart before God's tribunal seat. Those that are saved, it hath these effects in them that I have named. And if you ask how they know whether the word be the word? A man may answer, I have found it to be so, raising me up, comforting me, and strengthening me. I had perished in my affliction if the word had not raised me. Principles are proved, you know, from experience, for they have nothing above them. There is no other principle

---

[1] The first was under Nero, AD 64; the second under Domitian, 95; the third under Trajan, 100; the fourth under Adrian, 118; the fifth under Severus, 197; the sixth under Maximinus, 235; the seventh under Decius, more bloody than any preceding, 249; the eighth under Valerian, 257; the ninth under Aurelian, 272; and the tenth under Diocletian, which lasted ten years, 302.

[2] 'Idiot.' The word as used by Sibbes means a private person, and not at all, as now, a fatuous person.

to prove the word, but experience from the working of it. How know you the light to be the light, but by itself, and that fire is hot, but by itself? Principles prove themselves only by experience; and this principle is so proved by itself, that there is no child of God but can say by experience, that the word is the word.

6. *If a man might go to reason, one might bring that which could not be easily answered for the satisfaction of an atheist.* Let him but grant there is a God, he will grant one thing in religion or another. But let him grant there is a God and a reasonable creature, then there must be a service, a religion; and this service must be according to some rules prescribed; for the superior will not be served as the inferior pleaseth. He must discover what good the superior intendeth, and what duties he expects. This must be revealed in some word. God and the reasonable creature, and religion, make a necessity of a word, and that must be the word we have, or another; and what word in the world is probable to be the word but this?

Objection. You will say it may be corrupt.

Answer. The Jews looked to the Old Testament, that it should not be corrupted; for they knew every syllable in it, and preserved every letter. It is one part of their superstition, and God blesseth that superstition to take away all such cavils. For the New Testament the Jews cared not for; but heretics on their side watch over it that there should be no corruption; they will so observe one another. But what are these reasons to those which the soul of a gracious Christian knoweth by the operation of the word upon the heart?

Use 1. And, therefore, *let us regard it as the word of God*; hear it as the word of God; read it as the word of God. A company of profane wretches you shall have, the scums and basest of the people, that will discourse, and to grace their discourse, they must have Scripture phrases; but whose word is it? It is the word of the great God. Eglon was a heathen king, and yet when a message came from God, he arose up and made obeyance,[1] Judges 3:20. We should never read the word but with reverence, considering whose book it is, and that we must be judged by it another day.

Use 2. If it be the word, I beseech you consider what we say, and *know that God will make every part of it good*. There shall not a jot of it fail, nothing of it shall miscarry. God speaketh all these words. And, therefore, if you be blasphemers, you shall not carry it away guiltless. God hath said it. If you continue not to obey, you are under God's curse. Unless you repent you shall perish. Every threat God will make good. You must repent and get into Christ, else perish eternally. God hath said it, and we may confirm it in the unfolding and reading of it. The time is coming for the execution of it, and then God is peremptory. Now God waiteth our leisure, and entreateth us, but if we will not repent, we shall have that arrow in our sides that will never be gotten out till we die in hell. Whose sins are condemned in Scripture, they are condemned by God; and whom we shut heaven to, by opening the Scriptures, God will shut heaven to. The opening of the Scriptures is the opening of heaven. If the Scripture saith, a man that liveth in such a

---

[1] This interpretation of the 'rising up' of Eglon anticipates Bishop Patrick *in loc.*

sin shall not be saved, heaven shall be shut to him; he is in a state of death, he is strucken, and remaineth in danger till he repenteth. How many live in sins against conscience, that are under the guilt and danger of their sins. They be wounded, they be struck by the word. There is a threat against their sins, although it be not executed; and they be as much in danger of eternal death as a condemned traitor, only God suffers them to live, that they may make their peace. They have blessed times of visitation. Oh, make use of it! It is the word of God; and know that God will make every part of his word good in threats as well as in promises.

Use 3. Take occasion from hence likewise to shame ourselves for our infidelity[1] in the promises. When we are in any disconsolate estate, we are in Job's case. Being in trouble, the consolation of the Almighty seemed light to him, Job. 15:11. These be the comforts of God. When we come to comfort some, though the sweet promises of the gospel be opened, yet they do not consider them as being the word, the consolations of the Almighty, and therefore they seem light to them. But it should not be so. Consider they be the comforts of the word, and therefore we should hear them with faith, labour to affect[2] them, and shame ourselves. Is this God's word that giveth this direction, that giveth this comfort, and shall I not regard it? Is it the consolation of the Almighty, and shall not I embrace it? Therefore we should be ashamed, not to be more affected with the heavenly sweet things promised of God than we are.

A man that refuseth heavenly comforts to embrace comforts below, how should he reflect upon himself with

[1] That is, 'disbelief', or 'unbelief'.
[2] That is, to 'love' them.

shame? Hath God promised such things, God that cannot lie? and shall I lose my hope of all these glorious things, for the enjoying of the pleasures of sin for a season? I profess myself to be a Christian, where is my faith? where is my hope? A man must acknowledge either I have no faith; for if I had faith believing God speaking these excellent things, I would not venture my loss of them to get the enjoyment of poor temporary things here, for the good things promised in another world. Labour, therefore, to bring men's hearts to believe the word, and desire God to seal it to our souls that it is so.

Means. I will give one direction. *Labour for the Spirit of God, that writ the word, that indited the word.* Beg of God to seal to our souls that it is the word, and that he would sanctify our hearts to be suitable to the word, and never rest till we can find God by his Spirit seasoning our hearts, so that the relish of our souls may suit to the relish of divine truths, that when we hear them we may relish the truth in them, and may so feel the work of God's Spirit, that we may be able to say, he is our God. And when we hear of any threatening, we may tremble at it, and any sin discovered, we may hate it. For unless we, by the Spirit of God, have something wrought in us suitable to the word, we shall never believe the word to be the word. And therefore pray the Lord, by his Spirit to frame our hearts to be suitable to divine truths, and so frame them in our affections, that we may find the word in our joy, in our love, in our patience, that all may be seasoned with the word of God. When there is a relish in the word, and in the soul suitable to it, then a man is a Christian indeed to purpose. Till then men will apostatize, turn papist, turn atheist, or anything, because there is a distance between the soul and the word. The word is not engrafted into the soul. They do not know the word to be the word by arguments fetched from the word, and therefore they fall from the power of the word. But if we will not fall from divine truths, get truth written in the heart, and our hearts so seasoned by it, and made so harmonious and suitable to it, that we may embrace it to death, that we may live and die in it.

To go on:

'*In that day shall it be said, Lo, this is our God; we have waited for him.*'

Here is a gracious promise, that shutteth up all spoken before. He spake of great things before. And now here is a promise of a day, wherein he will make all things promised, good to the soul of every believing Christian.

'*In that day it shall be said, This is our God; we have waited for him; he will save us.*'

It is an excellent portion of Scripture to shew the gracious disposition that the Spirit of God will work in all those that embrace the gracious promises of God. The time shall come when they shall say, 'Lo, this is our God; we have waited for him, and now we enjoy him.'

The points considerable are these:

1. First of all by supposition that there be *glorious excellent things promised to the people of God*; rich and precious promises of feasting, of taking away the veil, of conquest over death by victory, of wiping away tears and removing rebukes. Great things, if we go no farther than my text.

2. Secondly, *these have a day when they shall be performed*, which is not presently; for the end of a promise is to

support the soul till the performance. God doth not only reserve great things for us in another world, but to comfort us in the way, doth reach out to us promises to comfort us till we come thither. There is a time when he will perform them, and not only a time, but there are likewise promises of performance. At that time the promises of these great things shall be performed.

3. The next thing is, *that God will stir up in his children a disposition suitable*. That is, the grace of waiting. As great things were promised before, so the soul hath a grace fit for it. 'We have waited for thee.'

4. And as they wait for them, while they are in performing, so they shall enjoy them. 'We have waited for thee, and we will be glad in thy salvation.' We shall so enjoy them, that we shall joy in them. Good things, when they be enjoyed, they be joyed in.

5. Again, 'we shall rejoice in our salvation, we shall glory in our God.' After they be a while exercised in waiting, then cometh performance, then they be enjoyed, and *they be enjoyed with joy, in glorying in God*. For that is the issue of a Christian, when he hath what he would enjoy, when he enjoyeth it with joy, when the fruit of it is that God hath his glory, and therefore the heart can rejoice in his salvation.

Then there is a day, as for the exercising of his people here by waiting, so there is a day of performing promises. 'In that day.' That is, a day of all days. When that day cometh, then all prophecies and promises shall be accomplished to the uttermost.

But before that great day, there is an intermediate performance of promises assisted by waiting, to drop comfort to us by degrees. He reserveth not all to that day. There be lesser days before that great day. As at the first coming of Christ, so at the overthrow of antichrist, the conversion of the Jews, there will be much joy. But that is not that day. These days make way for that day. Whensoever prophecies shall end in performances, then shall be a day of joying and glorying in the God of our salvation forever. And therefore in the Revelations where this Scripture is cited, Rev. 21:4, is meant the conversion of the Jews, and the glorious estate they shall enjoy before the end of the world. 'We have waited for our God,' and now we enjoy him. Aye, but what saith the church there? 'Come, Lord Jesus, come quickly.' There is yet another, 'Come, Lord,' till we be in heaven. So that though intermediate promises be performed here, yet there is another great day of the Lord to be performed, which is specially meant here.

6. The last thing considerable in the words is the manner of expression. They are expressed full of life, and with repetition, to make them sure and more certain, 'In that day it shall be said, This is our God; we have waited for him; he shall save us.' He bringeth them in speaking these words of affection.

Indeed, when we come to enjoy the performance of God's gracious promises, if we should live to see the fulness of the Gentiles come, and Jews called, we should speak of it again and again. Affections are large, and few expressions will not serve for large affections. It will be no tautology to say, 'This is our God; we have waited for him.'

Beloved, times are yet to come which may much affect the hearts of the children of God. Howsoever we may not live to see the performance of these things, yet we shall all live to see that day of judgment, and then we shall say, 'This is our God; we have waited for him.' We now see God in the promises, and then we shall see him 'face to face,' whom we have waited for in the promises, and we shall see him in heaven forever.

'Lo, this is our God; we have waited for him.' While we live here we are in state of waiting, we are under promises, and a condition under promises is a waiting condition; a condition of performance is an enjoying condition. We are in a waiting condition till our bodies be raised out of the grave; for when we die we wait for the resurrection of our bodies. We may say as Jacob when he was dying, 'I have waited for thy salvation.' We are in a waiting condition till body and soul be joined together at the day of judgment forever.

And there we should labour to have those graces that are suitable for this condition. The things we wait for are of so transcending excellency, as glory to come, that they cannot be waited for, but[1] the Spirit, by the things waited for, fitteth us to wait for them. A man cannot wait for glory of soul and body, but the Spirit that raiseth up faith to believe, and hope to wait, will purge, and fit, and prepare him for that glorious condition. 'He that hath this hope purifieth himself, as he is pure,' 1 John 3:3. Oh, it is a quickening waiting, and a purging waiting. It is efficacious by the Spirit to fit and purify his soul suitable to that glorious condition he waits for. Where that is not, it is but a conceit. A very slender apprehension of the glory to come will make men better. He that hath hope of heaven and happiness under glory, it will make him suitable to the place he looketh for.

---

[1] That is, 'unless.'

Sermon 8

*He shall swallow up death in victory; and the Lord God will
wipe away tears from off all faces; and the rebukes of his
people shall he take away from off all the earth: for the
Lord hath spoken it. And it shall be said in that day, Lo,
this is our God; we have waited for him, and he will save
us: this is the Lord; we have waited for him, we will be
glad and rejoice in his salvation.*

– Isaiah 25:8, 9

To come closer to the particulars. 'It shall be said in that
day, Lo, this is our God.' The mouth of the Lord hath spoken
gracious things before, hath promised a feast, and an excellent feast. God's manner is first of all to give promises to
his church. Why? His goodness cometh from his goodness,
his goodness of grace cometh from his goodness of nature.
'He is good and doth good! Now the same goodness of
disposition which we call bounty, that reserveth heaven
and happiness for us in another world, the same goodness
will not suffer us to be without all comfort in this world,
because the knowledge and revelation of the glory to
come hath much comfort in it. Therefore in mercy he not
only intendeth performance of glory, but out of the same
fountain of goodness he intendeth to reveal whatsoever is
good for his church in the way to glory. So that promises
of good come from the same goodness of God by which

he intendeth heaven. For what moved God to come out of that hidden light, that no man can come into, and discover himself in his Son? The word in his promises to reveal his mind to mankind, and make known what he will have us to do, and what he will do to us. But only his goodness is the cause of all. And therefore the end of promises in God's intention is to comfort us in the way to heaven, that we may have something to support us. They are *promissa, quasi præmissa*. They are promises and premises, and sent before the thing itself.

Now here it cometh that the glory to come is termed the joy of heaven and the glorious estate to come. 'You have need of patience, that you may get the promises.' Heaven and happiness is called the promises, because we have them assured in promises. The blessings of the New Testament are called promises; as the children of the promise, yea, the heirs of glory; because all is conveyed by a promise, therefore all happiness is conveyed by a promise.

Now the promises are of good things. They are for the spring of them, free, from God's free goodness; for the measure of them, full; for the truth of them, constant, even as God himself that promiseth. And therefore we may well build upon them.

Use. Before I go any farther, I beseech you let us account the promises of the good we have *to be our best treasure, our best portion, our best riches*, for they be called precious promises, 2 Pet. 1:4; not only because they be precious in themselves, but because they are from the precious love of God in Christ to us. They are likewise for precious things. They are laid hold of by precious faith, as the Scripture calleth them, and therefore they are precious promises. Let us not only account of our riches that we have; for what is that we have, to what we speak of, to that we have in promise? A Christian is rich in reversion,[1] rich in bills and obligations. Christ hath bound himself to him, and he can sue him out when he pleaseth. In all kinds of necessity, he can sue God for good. He can go to God and say, 'Remember thy promise, Lord, wherein thou hast caused me thy servant to trust,' Psa. 119:49; and can bind God with his own word.

But I take this only in passage as the foundation of what I am to speak.

From the mouth of God you see the great promises delivered; and now we have waited for them. That which answereth promises is expectation and waiting.

The second thing, therefore, between the promises, wherein God is a debtor, and the performance, is, that *there is a long time, a long day*. Oftentimes God takes a long day for performing of his promise, as four hundred years Abraham's posterity went to be in Egypt. And it was four thousand years from the beginning of the world till the coming of Christ, which was the promise of promises, the promise of the seed, a great long day. And therefore Christ is said to come in 'the latter end of the world.' Abraham had promise of a son, but it was not performed till he was an old man. Simeon had a promise to see Christ in the flesh, but he was an old man, ready to yield up the ghost, before it was performed. God taketh a long day for his promises;

---

[1] A legal term referring to the right of succession or future possession or enjoyment of an estate.

long to us, not to him, 'for to him a thousand years are but as one day.'

Reason 1. The promises of God are long in performing; for *to exercise our faith and our dependence to the full*;

Reason 2. *To take us off from the creature*; and

Reason 3. *To endear the things promised to us*, to set the greater price upon them when we have them. Many other reasons may be given, if I intended to enlarge myself in that point. A Christian hath a title to heaven. As soon as he is a Christian, he is an heir to heaven. Perhaps he may live here twenty or forty years more before God takes him up to glory. Why doth he defer it so long?

Reason 4. The reason is, *God will fit us for heaven by little and little*, and will perfume us as Esther was perfumed before she must come to Ahasuerus, Esth. 2:12. There were many weeks and months of perfuming. So God will sweeten and fit us for heaven and happiness. It is a holy place; God a holy God. Christ is that holy one; and for us to have ever-lasting communion with God and Christ in so holy a place, requireth a great preparation. And God, by deferring it so long, will mortify our affections by little and little, and will have us die to all base things here in affection before we die indeed. David had title to the kingdom as soon as ever he was anointed; but David was fitted to be an excellent king, indeed, by deferring the performance of the promise till afterward. So in our right and title and possession of heaven, there is a long time between.

Our Saviour Christ was thirty-four years before he was taken up to heaven, because he was to work our salvation. And he was willing to suspend his glory for such a time, that he might do it; to suspend his glory due to him from the first moment of his conception. For by virtue of the union, glory was due to him at the first; but because he had taken upon him to be a Mediator, out of love he would suspend his glory due to him, that he might suffer. And so God, by way of conformity, will suspend the glory due to us, that we may be conformed to Christ. Though we have right to heaven as soon as we are born,[1] yet God will suspend the full performance of it; because he will by correction and by length of time subdue by little and little that which maketh us unconformable to our head.

And can we complain for any deferring of heaven when we are but conformed to our glorious head, who was content to be without heaven so long?

But to go on. As there be gracious and rich promises, and they have long time of performance to us, and 'hope deferred makes the soul languish,' Prov. 13:12; so God vouchsafeth a spirit to fit that expectation of his, a spirit of hope and waiting. And this waiting hath something perfect in it, and something imperfect. It is a mixed condition. There is good, because there is a promise; for a promise is the declaration of God's will concerning good. But because it is a promise of a thing not performed, there is an imperfection. So there is a mixture in the promise, and a mixture in the grace. Hope and expectation and waiting is an imperfect grace. That there be glorious things, it is perfection of good; that we have them not in possession, that is the imperfection. So that hope is something, but it is not possessed; a promise is something, but it is not the performance; a seed is something, but it is not the plant.

[1] That is, 'born again.'

THE GLORIOUS FEAST OF THE GOSPEL

Thus God mixeth our condition here of perfection and imperfection. He will have us in state of imperfection, that we may not think ourselves at home in our country, when we are but in our way. Therefore he will have us in a state of imperfection, that we may long homeward; yet he will have it a state of good, that we may not sink in the way.

And not only promises; for in the way to heaven God keeps not all for heaven. He lets in drops of comfort oftentimes in the midst of misery. He doth reveal himself more glorious and sweet than at other times. There is nothing reserved for us in another world, but we have a beginning, a taste, an earnest of it here, to support us till we come to the full possession of what remaineth. We shall have full communion of saints there; we have it here, in the taste of it. We know what it is to be acquainted with them that be gracious spirits. We have praising of God forever there. We know the sweetness of it here in the house of God, which made David desire this one thing, 'that he might dwell in the house of God, to visit the beauty of God,' etc., Psa. 27:4. There we shall have perfect peace; here we have inward peace, unspeakable and glorious, 'a peace that passeth understanding,' Phil. 4:7, in the beginning of it. There we shall have joy without all mixture of contrariety; here we have joy, 'and joy unspeakable and full of glory,' 1 Peter 1:8. There is nothing in heaven that is perfect, that is sweet, and good, and comfortable, but we have a taste and earnest of it here. The Spirit will be all in all there; there is something of it in us now. More light in our understandings, more obedience in our wills, more and more love in our affections, and it is growing more and more.

And therefore all is not kept for time to come; we have something beginning here besides promises. There is some little degrees of performance. So that the state between us and heaven is a state mixed of good and imperfection.

Now God hath fitted graces suitable to that condition, and that is expectation or waiting, a fit grace and a fit disposition of soul from[1] imperfect condition, that is afterwards to be perfected; for fruition is the condition of perfect happiness, not of waiting; for waiting implieth imperfection.

This waiting carrieth with it almost all graces. Waiting for better times in glory to come, it hath to support it. It is a carriage of soul that is supported with many graces. For, first, we wait for that we believe. We have a spirit of faith to lead to it. And then we hope before we wait, and hope is the anchor of the soul, that stayeth the soul in all the waves and miseries of the world. It is the helmet that keeps off all the blows. This hope issues from faith; for what we believe, we hope for the accomplishment of it.

So that all graces make way for waiting, or accompany it. The graces that accompany the waiting for good things in time to come are *patience*, to endure all griefs between us and the full possession of heaven; then *longsuffering*, which is nothing else but patience lengthened, because troubles are lengthened, and the time is lengthened. So there is patience, and patience lengthened, which we call longsuffering; and then, together with patience and longsuffering, there is *contentment*, without murmuring at the dispensation of God; something in the soul that he would have it to be so. He that hath a heart to rise, because he hath not what

[1] Qu. 'for'?

he would have, he doth not wait with that grace of waiting that issueth from a right spring.

God reserveth joy for the time to come, for our home. We should be content to have communion with God and the souls of perfect men; and not murmur though God exerciseth us with many crosses here. And therefore the Scripture calleth it a *silence*, 'In silence and in hope shall be your strength,' Isa. 30:15. The soul keepeth silence to God in this waiting condition, and this silence quells all risings in the soul presently; as David, 'My soul kept silence unto the Lord,' Psa. 39:2. It will still all risings of the heart, issuing from a resignation of the soul to God, to do as he will have us to do. So it implieth patience and longsuffering, contentment, holy silence, without murmuring and repining.

And then it implies *watchfulness* over ourselves, till we come to the full accomplishment of the promises, that we carry not ourselves unworthily in the meantime; that we should not spend the time of our waiting in wickedness, to fetch sorrow from the devil, and the world to comfort us, or to be beholden to Satan. This is no waiting, but murmuring and rebellion, when in crosses and discomforts we cannot be content, but must be beholden to the devil, so there must be watchfulness; and not only so, but *fruitfulness* in waiting. For he waits that waiteth in doing good, that waiteth in observance. He waiteth for his master's coming, that is doing his duty all the time in a fruitful course of observance and obedience; else it is no waiting. Waiting is not merely a distance of time, but a filling up of that time with all gracious carriage, with obedience, and with silence, with longsuffering and contentment, and watchfulness [that] we take not any ill course, and observance, and with fruitfulness, that we may fill up times of waiting till performance, with all the graces, that we may have communion with God.

It is another manner of grace than the world thinks. What is the reason of all the wickedness of the world, and barrenness, and voluptuousness, but because they have not learned to wait? They hear of good things, and precious things promised; but they would have present payment, they will have something in hand. As Dives, 'Son, son, thou hast had thy good things here,' Luke 16:25, they will have their goods things here. And what is the reason of wickedness, but because they will have present pleasures of sins? We must prefer the afflictions of Christ before the pleasures of sin, Heb. 11:25. Now that shortness of spirit to have reward here is the cause of all sin. They have no hope, nor obedience, nor expectation to endure the continuance of diuturnity.[1] Where then is patience, and hope, and contentment?

The character of a Christian is, that he is in a waiting condition, and hath the grace of waiting. Others will have the pleasures of sin, their profits and contentments, else they will crack their consciences, and sell Christ, God, heaven; and all.

A Christian, as he hath excellent things above the world, so he hath the grace of expectation, and all the graces that store up and maintain that expectation till the performance come.

And therefore it is an hard thing to be a good Christian, another thing than the world taketh it to be. For mark, I beseech you, what is between us and heaven, that we must go through, if ever we will come there. Between us and

[1] That is, 'long continuance.'

heaven, the thing promised, there be many crosses to be met withal, and they must be borne, and borne as a Christian should do. 'Through many afflictions we must enter into the kingdom of heaven,' Acts 14:22. Besides crosses, there be scandalous offences, that be enough to drive us from profession of religion, without grace. Sometimes good men by their failings, and fallings out, they fall into sin, and fall out; and that is a scandal to wicked men. Oh, say they, who would be of this religion, when they cannot agree among themselves? This is a great hindrance and stop. It is a scandal and rub in the way, not so much in themselves. We are full of scandal ourselves, catch at anything that we may except against the best ways. There is a root of scandal in the hearts of all, because men will not go to hell without reason.

Now because we are easy to take offence, rather than we will be damned without reason, it is not easy to hold out. Besides this, Satan plies it with his temptations from affliction, and from scandal; he amplifies these things in the fancy. Who would be a Christian? You see what their profession is. And so he maketh the way the more difficult.

And then again, look at our own disposition to suffer, to hold out, to fix. There is an unsettledness, which is a proper[1] infirmity in our natures since the fall. We love variety, we are inconstant, and cannot fix ourselves upon the best things, and we are impatient of suffering anything. We are not only indisposed to do good, but more indisposed to suffer any ill. The Spirit must help us over all this, which must continue all our life long. Till we be in heaven, something or other will be in our way. Now the Spirit of God must help

[1] That is, 'natural.'

us over all these afflictions. We shall never come to heaven to overcome afflictions, and scandals, and temptation, which Satan plies us here withal. And then to overcome the tediousness of time, this needeth a great deal of strength. Now this grace of expectance doth all. And therefore it is so oftentimes stood upon in Scripture. In Isaiah, and in the Psalms, how often is it repeated; Psa. 37:7. 'Wait on the Lord; if he tarry, wait thou.' The Lord will wait for them that wait for him; and it is the character in Scripture of a Christian. Moses, he saith, such as waited for the consolation of Israel, Gen. 49:18, before Christ came in the flesh, such a one is one that 'waiteth for the consolation of Israel,' Luke 2:25. To have a gracious disposition, and a grace of waiting was the character of good people. Now since the coming of Christ, the character of the New Testament is, to wait for Christ's appearance. 'There is a crown of glory for me, and not only for me, but for all them that love his appearance,' 2 Tim. 4:8. That is an ingredient in waiting, when we love the thing we wait for. And so Titus 2:12, 'The grace of God that teacheth to deny ungodliness and worldly lusts, and to live holily, and justly, and soberly in this present evil world, looking for and waiting for this glorious appearing of Jesus Christ.'

So that looking with the eye of the soul partly on the first coming of Christ, which was to redeem our souls, and partly upon the second, which is to redeem our bodies from corruption, and to make both soul and body happy, it makes a man a good Christian. For the grace of God on the first, teacheth us to deny ungodliness; and looking for Christ's appearing, maketh us zealous of good works. You have scarce any epistle, but you have time described for looking for the coming of Christ, as Jude, 'Preserve yourselves in the love of God, and wait for the coming of Christ.' So that as there be gracious promises, and a long day for them, God vouchsafeth grace to wait for the accomplishment of them.

Now as God giveth grace to wait, so he will perform what we wait for; as they say here, 'We have waited.' That is the speech of enjoying. God will at length make good what he hath promised; and what his truth hath promised, his power will perform. Goodness inclineth to make a promise, truth speaks it, and power performeth it, as you shall see here.

'*We have waited*,' etc.

In God there is a mouth of truth, a heart of pity, and an hand of power. These three meeting together, make good whatsoever is promised; 'He will fulfil the desires of them that fear him,' Psa. 145:19. The desires that God hath put into his children, they be kindled from heaven; and he will satisfy them all out of his bowels of pity and compassion. He will not suffer the creature to be always under the rack of desire, under the rack of expectation, but he will fulfil the desire of them that fear him. And therefore learn this for the time to come.

Though we wait, God will perform whatsoever we wait for. And therefore, 'Lo, we have waited for him.' As there is a time of promising, so there is a time of performing; as there is a seedtime, so there is a time of harvest. There is a succession in nature, and a succession in grace; as the day followeth the night, and the Sabbath the week, and the jubilee such a term of years; and as the triumph followeth the war; and as the consummation of marriage followeth contract; so it is a happy and glorious condition, above all conditions here on earth. Therefore in this text you have not only the seedtime of the Christian (we may sow in tears, and in expectation, as in sowing), but here is likewise the harvest of a Christian. As there is time of sowing, so there is time of reaping; as time of waiting, so of enjoying. We have waited, and now, lo, we have what we waited for.

But why doth not the Holy Ghost set down a certain time, but leaveth it indefinite, 'In that day.' God keeps times and seasons in his own power; the point of time in general he leaveth it. There is a day; but the point and moment of time he keepeth in his own power. It is enough to know there is a day, and a day that will come in the best season. God's time is the best time. When judgments were threatened upon the wicked, they say, 'Let us eat, and drink, for tomorrow we shall die,' 1 Cor. 15:32. So Saul, 'Tomorrow thou shalt die,' 1 Sam. 28:19, and was he the better? So where there is a certain time of God's coming in judgment, godly men would not be the worse, and wicked men never the better. Therefore God reserveth it indefinite, 'In that day.'

There is a day, and it is a glorious day, a day of all days, a day that never will have night, a day that we should think of every day, 'That day,' by way of excellency. And before that day there be particular days in this world, wherein God sheweth himself, and fulfils the expectation of his children, to cherish the grand expectation of life everlasting. As in times of trouble they expect of God, and wait for deliverance in God's time, and they must be able to say, 'Lo, we have waited.' Because it is a beginning and pledge of the great performance that shall be consummate at that great day, and of all the miseries that shall then be removed; so there is a day when the Jews shall be converted, and the fulness of the Gentiles brought in, and the man of sin discovered, and consumed by the breath of Christ. And when the church of God seeth them, they may say, 'Lo, we have waited for the Lord,' and lo, he is come; that we looked for is now fulfilled. So that God reserveth not the fulfilling of all the promises to the great day of all days, but even in this life he will have a 'that day.'

And it were very good for Christians in the passages of their lives to see how God answereth their prayers, and delivereth them. Let them do as the saints in the Old Testament, that gave names to places where they saw God, as Peniel, Gen. 32:30, he shall see God, and Abraham, 'God will be seen in the mount,' Gen. 22:14. So Samson and others, they gave names to places where they had deliverance, that they might be moved to be thankful. A Christian taketh in all the comforts of this life to believe the things of the last great day. 'Lo, we have waited for him.'

That shall be a time of sight and fruition, of full power and full joy, which is reserved for heaven; then we shall say, 'Lo! behold, this is the Lord.' The more we see God here, the more we shall see him hereafter. There be many ways of seeing, so as to say, 'Lo, this is the Lord!' We may say, from the poorest creature, 'Lo, this is the Lord!' Here are beams of his majesty in the works of his justice and mercy, 'Lo, here is the Lord!' 'The Lord hath brought mighty things to pass, the Lord is marvellous loving to his children.' 'Behold and see the salvation of the Lord!' We may say, 'Lo, here'; and see something of God in every creature. No creature but hath something of God. The things that have but mere being have something of God; but the things that have life have more of God. And so in some there is more, in some less of God.

But in the church of God specially, we may see his going in the sanctuary. Lo, this God hath done for his church. And in the sacraments, we may say, I have seen the Lord, and felt the Lord in his ordinance by his Holy Spirit. We do all this before we come to see him in heaven. But that is not meant specially.

We shall say, 'Lo, this is the Lord!' when we shall see him in heaven. All sight here leadeth to that sight. Faith hath a sight here, but it is in the word and sacrament, and so imperfect; but the sight in heaven is immediate and perfect, and therefore opposed to faith. We live by faith, and not by sight. In heaven we shall live by sight; not that we live not by sight here in some degree, for the lesser sight leadeth to the greater sight. But in comparison of sight in heaven, there is no sight. The Scripture speaketh of sight of God comparatively. Moses 'saw God,' that is, more than any other; and Jacob 'saw God,' that is, comparatively more than before, but not fully and wholly. We can apprehend him, but not comprehend him, as they say. We may see something of him, but not wholly. But in heaven we shall have another sight of God, and then we shall say, 'Lo, this is the God we have waited for!' We shall see Christ face to face.

Beloved, that is the sight indeed. And if ye will ask me whether we shall see God then or no, consider what I said before. This is the God we have waited for in obedience, and fruitfully.

If we shall be ravished with the sight of God, surely if we see him here, we may see him there. We see him with the eye of faith, we see him in the ordinance, we have some sight of God that the world hath not. God discovereth himself to his children, more than to the world; and therefore they say, 'Thou revealest thyself to us, not unto the world,' John 14:22. A Christian wonders that God should reveal his love, and mercy, and goodness to him, more than to others. And therefore, if we belong to God, and shall see him hereafter, we must see him now. As we may see him, we must have some knowledge of him. And if we see God any way, all things in the world will be thought of no request, in comparison of the communion of God in Christ, as, 'We have seen the Lord, and what have we to do with idols?' Hosea 14:8. The soul that hath seen Christ, grows in detestation of sin, and loatheth all things in comparison.

And then, again, if we shall ever see God in glory, in this glorious and triumphing manner, 'This is the Lord,' this sight is a changing sight. There is no sight of God, but it changeth, and alters to the likeness of God, when he calls to look up to him, and he looks on us in favour and mercy. The best fruit of his favour is grace, of peace, and joy, for these be beams that issue from him, grace, as beams from the sun. But wherever God looks with any favour, there is a conformity to Christ, a gracious, humble, pitiful, merciful, obedient disposition, which is an earnest of the Spirit of Christ.

And there is a study of purity, of a refined disposition from the pollutions of the world. 'The pure in heart shall see God,' Matt. 5:8. They that hope to see God forever in heaven, will study that purity that may dispose and fit them for heaven. And there is such a gracious influence in it, that they that hope for heaven, the very hope must needs help to purify them.

As there is grace suitable to waiting, so there is an influence from the things hoped for, to give vigour to all grace. As all the graces of a Christian fit and enable him for heaven, so hope of heaven yields life to all grace. There is a mutual influence into these things. God vouchsafeth discovery of these glorious things, to help us to wait, to be patient, and fruitful, and abundant in the work of the Lord. And the more we wait fruitfully, and patiently, and silently, the more we see of heaven. So that as in nature, the seed bringeth the tree, and the tree the seed; so in the things of God, one thing breeds another, and that breeds that again. So that waiting and grace fit us for heaven, and the thought of heaven puts life and vigour into all the graces that fit us for heaven. What is our faith to those glorious things we shall see hereafter? What is patience, but for consideration of that? What is hope, but for the excellency of the object of hope? And what were enduring of troubles, if something were not in heaven to make amends for all? They help us to come to glory, and the lively, hopeful thoughts of those things, animate and enliven all the graces that fit for heaven. If ever we shall hereafter possess heaven, and say, 'Lo, this is he we have waited for,' we must see him here, so as to undervalue all things, to see him with a changing sight; for the object of glory cannot be revealed, but it will stir up a disposition suitable to glory. If this be not, never hope for a sight of him in heaven.

And therefore let me entreat and beseech you, with the apostle Paul, to 'look to the end,' look to the main chance that can come in this world, and that shall come hereafter. It is wisdom to look to the end. A man that buildeth an house will think of the end, that is, dwelling and habitation, that he propoundeth. We are for everlasting communion with God; we are to be perfect, as in grace, so in glory. Heaven is our element; we rest not till then, – we are in motion till then, – that being our station. Then think often of this, never to rest in any intermediate condition, because we are in waiting till we come to that condition. Let us so carry ourselves, that we may say, this we waited for; it is the glory we expected. It is our wisdom often to have the end of our lives in our eyes, that we may be helped to wait patiently, cheerfully, and comfortably, till the consummation come, when all promises shall end in performance, when all that is ill and imperfectly good shall be removed – a consumption of ill, and a consummation of all good.

Oh, have that day in our eyes, that day of all days, and the very thoughts of it will fit us for the day. The thoughts of our end will fit and stir us up to all means tending to that end. Physic[1] is good, if it tend to health. The very thoughts of that prescribes order and means. We read, 'Seek the kingdom of heaven first, and all other things shall be added to you,' Matt. 6:33. The thought of the end prescribes order to all means, and it prescribes measure, 'How to use the world, as though I used it not,' 1 Cor. 7:31, for the thoughts of my end stir me up to use all our courses suitable to that end. And therefore the best wisdom in Christians is often to prefix the end, and to be content in no grace nor comfort, as it is in a way of imperfection, but to look upon every grace, every comfort, every good, as it tends to perfection. David desired not to dwell in the house of God forever, because he would terminate his desire in the house of God here, but he aimeth at heaven. And so when the saints of God bound and terminate their desires and contentment, it is with reference to the last day, the rest of a Christian, beyond which they cannot go, even communion with God himself.

[1] That is, medicine.

Sermon 9

And it shall be said in that day, Lo, this is our God; we have waited for him, and he will save us: this is the Lord; we have waited for him, we will be glad and rejoice in his salvation.

– Isaiah 25:9

In the worst age of the church, that the church may not be swallowed up with fear, in the worst times, God doth prepare promises for his people. It was the case of our blessed Saviour himself to his poor disciples, that they might not be overwhelmed with sorrow. Therefore he addeth sacraments to passover, and the New Testament to the Old, and all to confirm faith, knowing that our hearts are very subject to be daunted.

The Lord promiseth here a feast of fat things, and all things pertaining to a feast, the best of the best, and removal of all that may hinder joy, as taking away the veil, which hinders them from the sight of it. And then death is swallowed up in victory, as it is already in our Head, who is gloriously triumphing in heaven; and then all tears shall be wiped from all faces. There is a vicissitude of things. They are now in a valley of tears, but it will not be always thus. Time shall come when all tears shall be wiped away, and the cause of all tears are sorrow. The rebukes of his people shall be taken away, the scandal that lieth upon the best things shall be taken away. The worst things go under a better representation, and the best things under a veil; but one day, as things are they shall be. The God of truth will have truth to be clear enough. And all this is sealed up with the highest authority, that admits of no contradiction. 'The Lord of hosts hath spoken it.'

We came the last day to these words, 'Lo, this is our God,' etc.; wherein we may consider first of all, *that God hath left to his church rich and precious promises*, such as is spoken of before: a feast, and removal of all hindrances whatsoever. He not only vouchsafeth heaven when we die, and eternal happiness; but in this world, in our way, he vouchsafes precious promises to support our faith, that we may begin heaven upon earth. What these promises are we shewed the last day.

The second observation was, in that God's people are here *in a state of expectation*, it shall be said, 'Lo, we have waited for him.' We are in a condition of waiting while we live in this world, because we are not at home. Our state requires waiting; heaven requires settledness and rest. There all appetites, all desires shall be satiated to the full. Our estate here is a passage to a better estate, and waiting is a disposition fit for such a condition.

And in this there is good and imperfection. Good, that we have something to wait for; imperfection, that we are to wait for it, that we have it not in fruition; and till we be in heaven we are in a state of waiting. In the Revelations, 'Come, Lord Jesus, come quickly,' Rev. 22:20, there is a glorious state of a church set forth; but while all is done, it hath not what it would have. We cannot be in such a state in the world; but there is place for a desire, namely, immediate and eternal communion with Christ in heaven. And therefore 'it shall be said in that day, Lo, this is our God; we have waited for him.'

I will add a little to this state of waiting before I go farther. God will not have our condition presently perfect, but have us continue in a state of waiting.

Reason 1. First of all, it is his pleasure that *we should live by faith*, and not by sight. We have sense and feeling of many things; he reserveth not all for heaven. How many sweet refreshments have we in the way! But the tenor of our life is by faith, and not by sight. God will have us in such a condition.

Reason 2. Again, *we are not fitted for sight of the glory to come here*. Our vessels are not capable of that glory. A few drops of that happiness so overcame Peter in the transfiguration, that he knew not himself,

Reason 3. God is so good to us that *he would have us enjoy the best at the last*. The sweeter is heaven, by how much the more difficult our way thither is. Heaven is heaven, and happiness is happiness, after a long time of waiting. For waiting enlargeth the capacity and desires of the soul to receive more; it commendeth the happiness afterwards. And therefore God keepeth the best for the last, because he will never interrupt the happiness of his children. When they be in heaven, there is a banishment of all cause of sorrow. He will have a distinction between the church militant and triumphant. He will train up his children here before he bringeth them to heaven. He will perfume his spouse, and make her fit for an everlasting communion with him in heaven.

The third thing is, that as there be promises, and these promises are not presently fulfilled, which put us in a state of waiting, *so God giveth grace to uphold in waiting.* Waiting is not an empty time, to wait so long, and no grace in the meantime; but waiting is a fitting time for that we are to receive afterwards.

We see in nature, in the winter, which is a dull time to the spring and harvest, and the times are very cold; yet it ripens and mellows the soil, and fits it for the spring. There is a great promotion of harvest in winter. It is not a mere distance of time. So between the promise and heaven itself, it is not a mere waiting time, and there is an end; but it is a time which is taken up by the Spirit of God in preparing the heart, in subduing all base lusts, and in taking us off from ourselves, and whatsoever is contrary to heaven. The time is filled up with a great deal of that which fits us for glory in heaven. The gracious God that fits us for heaven, and heaven for us, fits us with all graces necessary for that condition. As faith to believe, patience to wait for, and to depend on that which he seeth not, to be above sense; a grace of hope to wait for that which he believeth, to be an anchor to his soul in all conditions whatsoever. And then a grace of patience to wait meekly all the while. And then longsuffering, patience lengthened out. As the tediousness is long between us and heaven, so there be lengthening graces. We would have all presently, 'How long, Lord, how long?' Rev. 6:10. We are so short, even David and others; and therefore God giveth grace to hold out and lengthen our spiritual faith, and hope, and perseverance, and constant courage to encounter with all difficulties in the way. When the spirit of a man beholds heaven, and happiness, and God, it makes him constant, in some sort as the things he beholdeth, for the Spirit transformeth him to the object. Now, he beholds a constant covenant; and as faith looks upon a constant God, constant happiness, and constant promises, it frameth the soul suitable to the excellency of the object it layeth hold upon.

And then the Spirit of God in the way to heaven subdueth all evil murmurings and exceptions, in suffering us not to put forth our hands to any iniquity. Though we have not what we would have, he keeps us in a good and fruitful way; for to wait is not only to endure, but to endure in a good course, fitting us for happiness, till grace end in glory.

In the fourth place, *God will perform all his promises in time.* As the church saith here, 'This is the Lord; we have waited for him.' Now, he hath made good whatsoever he hath said.

To enlarge this point a little. As there is a time of waiting, so there will be a time when God's people shall say, 'Lo, this is the Lord, we have waited for him.' Why?

Reason 1. *God is Jehovah.* A full and pregnant word! A word of comfort and stay for the soul is this word Jehovah! He is a God that giveth a being to all things, and a being to his word, and therefore what he saith he will make good. He is Lord of his word. Every man's word is, as his nature, and power, and ability is, the word of a man, or the word of an honest man, but being the word of a God, he will make all good.

Reason 2. And then he will make all good, because *he is faithful.* God, he saith it, and he will do it.

Reason 3. You need no more reason *than pity to his people*, his bowels of compassion. The hearts of people would fail if he should stay too long. And therefore out of his bowels in his time, which is the best time, not only because he is faithful, but because he is loving and pitiful, he will make good all his promises. And then he will do it.

Reason 4. *For what is grace, but an earnest of that fulness we shall have in heaven?* What is peace here but an earnest of that peace in heaven? And what is joy here but an earnest of fulness of joy for evermore? And will God lose his earnest? Therefore we shall enjoy what God hath promised, and we expect, because we have the earnest. It is not a pledge only, for a pledge may be taken away, but an earnest, which is never taken away, but is made up in the full bargain. Grace is made up in glory, as beginnings are made up with perfection. Where God layeth a foundation, he will perfect it. Where God giveth the first-fruits, he will give the harvest.

But it will be a long time before, because he will exercise all grace to the uttermost. You see how Abraham was brought to the last. In the mountain God provideth for a sacrifice, when the knife was ready to seize on Isaac's throat, Gen. 22:12, 13.

We should answer with our faith God's dealing; that is, if God defer, let us wait, yea, wait to the uttermost, wait to death. He is our God to death, and in death, and forever. If God perform his promise at the worst, then, till we are at the lowest, we must wait.

And, therefore, one character of a child of God from others is this. Give me the present, saith the carnal, beastly man, the world; but God's people are content to wait. He knoweth what he hath in promise is better than what he hath in possession. The gleanings of God's people are better than the others' harvest. The other cannot wait, but must have present payment. God's child can wait, for he liveth by faith. And therefore we should learn patiently to wait for the performance of all God's promises.

And to direct a little in that, remember some rules, which every man may gather to himself, as,

1. *God's time is the best time. Deus est optimus arbiter opportunitatis*, the best discerner of opportunities. And 'in the mountain will God be seen.' Though he tarry long, he will come, and not tarry over long; and then all the strength of the enemy is with God. *Robur hostium apud Deum*. The strength of the enemy is in his hand; he can suspend it when he pleaseth.

2. Then, though God seems *to carry things by contrary ways to that he promiseth*, which makes waiting so difficult, yet he will bring things about at last. He promiseth happiness, and there is nothing but misery. He promiseth forgiveness, and opens the conscience to cry out of sin. Aye, but Luther's rule is exceeding good in this case. *Summa ars*, the greatest art of a Christian is, *credere credibilia*, etc., and *sperare dilata*, to hope for things a long time, and to believe God when he seemeth contrary to himself in his promise.

But though God doth defer, yet *in that day* he doth perform. It is set down indefinitely, for it is not fit we should be acquainted with the particular time. And therefore he saith, 'in that day.' He sets not down a particular time, but 'in that day,' wherein he meaneth to be glorious in the performance of his promise. There is a time, and a set time, and there is a short time, too, in regard of God, and a fit time. If the time were shorter than God hath appointed, then it were too short; if longer, too long. 'My times,' saith David, 'are in thy hands,' Psa. 31:15. If they were in the enemy's hands, we should never be out; if in our own, we would never enter; if in our friends', their goodwill would be more than their ability. 'But my times'; – he saith not, 'my time,' but – 'my times are in thy hands'; that is, my times of trouble and times of waiting. And it is well that they be in God's hands, for he hath a day, and a certain day, and a fit day to answer the waiting of all his people.

And when that day is come, you see how their hearts are enlarged, they will say, 'This is the Lord, we have waited for him.'

When God meaneth to perform his promise, either in this world or in the world to come, the world to come specially, when there shall be consummation of all promises, God shall enlarge the hearts of his people. 'This is the Lord; we have waited for him.' 'This is the Lord.' He repeats it again and again.

Our soul is very capable, being a spiritual substance; and then God shall fill the soul, and make it comprehend misery, or comprehend happiness, when every corner of the soul shall be filled; and then having bodies too, it is fit they should have a part; so the whole man shall express forth the justice or mercy of God.

For the nature of the thing, it cannot be otherwise. Every member of the body shall be fit to glorify God. What the psalmist saith of his tongue, 'Awake, my glory,' he may say of every member, Do thy office in glorifying the Lord, and rejoicing in the Lord. *Pectus facit disertos*. The heart makes a man eloquent and full. So the performance of any promise fills the heart so full of affections, the affections are so enlarged; and therefore we must not have affections to a court-kind of expressions, as they in old time, and the like court-eloquence, when men might not speak fully. But when joy possesseth the heart to the full, there be full expressions. 'This is the Lord, this is the Lord; let us rejoice in him.' And therefore there seemeth so many tautologies in the Psalms, though they be no tautologies, but mere exuberances of a sanctified affection.

Oh! beloved, what a blessed time will that be when this large heart of ours shall have that that will fill it; when the best parts of us, our understanding, will, and affections, shall be carried to that which is better and larger than itself, and shall be, as it were, swallowed up in the fulness of God. And that is the reason of the repetition of the word, 'This is the Lord, this is the Lord.'

And it followeth, 'We will rejoice and be glad in his salvation.' When a gracious heart is full of joy, how doth he express that joy? A wicked heart, when it is full of joy, is like a dirty river that runs over the banks, and carrieth a deal of filth with it, dirty expressions. But when a gracious heart expresseth itself, being full of joy, it expresseth itself in thanks and praises, in stirring up of others. 'Lo, this is our God; we will rejoice and be glad in his salvation.' 'Is any merry?' saith the apostle Saint James, 'let him sing,' James 5:13. God hath affections for any condition. 'Is a man in misery? let him pray.' This is a time of mourning. Doth God perform any promise, and so give cause of joy? let him sing. There is action for every affection, affection for every condition. And this may stir us up to begin the employment in heaven on earth here. We shall say so in heaven, 'Lo, this is the Lord; we have waited for him.'

For every performance of promises, be much in thankfulness. 'Our conversation is in heaven,' saith the apostle, Phil. 3:10. And what is the greatest part of a Christian's conversation, but in all things to give thanks. Here the holy church saith, their matter of praise was too big for their soul, and therefore they brake out in this manner. And so oftentimes a child of God. His heart is so full, that it is too big for his body in the expression of matter of praise. But it is his comfort that in heaven he shall have a large heart, answerable to the large occasion of praise. I will not enlarge myself in the common-place of thanksgiving.

In this condition we can never be miserable; for it springs from joy, and joy disposeth a man to thankfulness, and upon thankfulness there is peace, and can we be miserable in peace of conscience? Therefore, saith the apostle, 'In all things give thanks, and let your requests be made known to God,' Phil. 4:6; and what will follow upon that, when I have made known my requests, and paid my tribute of thanks? 'Then the peace of God which passeth understanding shall guide your mind,' Phil. 4:7. When we have paid to God the tribute we can pay him, then the soul, as having discharged a debt, is at peace. I have prayed to God, I have laid my petition in his bosom, I am not in arrearages for former favours, 'therefore the peace of God which passeth all understanding shall keep your hearts and minds.' Hannah had prayed once, went not away, but prayed again, 1 Sam. 2:1, *seq*. The happiness of heaven followeth the actions of heaven. Praisings being the main employment of heaven, the happiness and comfort of heaven followeth.

And howsoever these promises be fulfilled in heaven, yet they have a gradual performance on earth. For he speaks certainly of the state of the Jews yet to come, wherein there shall be accomplishment of all these promises.

'We have waited for him; he will save us.' Experience of God's performance stirs them up still to wait for him, and rejoice in his salvation. Experience stirs up hope. The beginning of a Christian, and midst, is to hope for the end; and surely our beginning should help the latter end! All a Christian's life should help the end. All former things should come in and help his latter.

Beloved, we are too backward that way to treasure up the benefit of experience. There be few of years but might make stories of God's gracious dealings with them, if all were kept; the comforts past, and for time to come, and all little enough. It was David's course, 'Thou art my God from my mother's womb, and upon thee have I hanged ever since I was born; fail me not when I am old,' Psa. 22:10. Go along with God's favours, and use them as arguments of future blessings. As former victories are helps to get the second victory, every former favour helpeth to strengthen our faith.

In the next, God is an inexhausted fountain, and when we have to deal with an infinite God, the more we take of him the more we offer him. It is no good plea to say, you have done courtesies, therefore do them still. But we cannot honour God more than from former experience to look for great things from the great God.

THE GLORIOUS FEAST OF THE GOSPEL

'We have waited for him, he will save us; we have waited for him, and we will rejoice in his salvation.' That which a child of God gives thanks for and rejoices in, and labours for, is more and more experience of his salvation. 'We will rejoice in his salvation.' There is not a stronger word in all the Scripture, not in nature. He doth not say rejoicing in this or that benefit, but in his salvation, that is, in deliverance from all evil. We will rejoice in his preservation, when he hath delivered us, we will rejoice in his advancement of us, and we will rejoice in his salvation. And therefore, when the wisdom of heaven would include all in one word, he useth the word Jesus, all happiness in that word, that pregnant, full word, a Saviour.

So that God's carriage towards his children is salvation. He is the God of salvation, or a saving God. And God sent his name from heaven, and the angels brought it, the name of Jesus. Therefore look to the full sense of it. We have a Saviour that will answer his name; as he is Jesus, so he will save his people from their sins, Matt. 1:21. And therefore we will rejoice in his salvation. God dealt with us like a God, when he delivered us from all misery, from all sins, and advanced us to all happiness that nature is capable of. As he said before, he will wipe away all tears from all faces, and take away the rebukes of all people. He will punish the wicked with eternal destruction. And if he advanceth a people he will be salvation, than which he can say no more.

And this sheweth that the children of God rejoice, more than in anything else, in salvation, because it is the salvation of God, and because God is salvation itself. Heaven were not heaven, if Jesus and God in our nature were not there. And therefore the apostle saith, 'I desire to depart,' not to be dissolved, 'and to be with Christ, for that is better.' The sight of God, specially in our nature, God the second person taking our nature, that we might be happy, will make us happy forever. In loving God, and joying in God, and enjoying God, makes full happiness; but that is not the cause of joy in heaven, but the cause of all is God's influence into us. Here in the world happiness is mediate, in God's revealing of himself to us by his Holy Spirit, in the use of means, in his dealings and deliverances, letting us see him by his grace, to see him, and joy and delight in him forever. It is no good love that resteth in any blessings of God for themselves. It is an harlotry affection to love the gift more than the giver. So the saints of God they do all desire to see him as they may, and to joy in God, and enjoy God himself, and to see God in our nature, and to be with him forever. Before he spake of a feast, and if the feast-maker be not there, what is all? In a funeral feast there is much cheer, but the feast-maker is gone. In heaven there is joy, but where is God, where is Christ, he that hath done so much, suffered so much for us, that hath taken possession of heaven, and keepeth a place for us there? What is heaven without him? Salvation, severed from him, is nothing.

We shall say when we are there, Lo, here is David, Abraham, St John, here the martyrs! Aye, but here is Christ, here is God, here is our Saviour, the cause of all, and the seeing of him in them, that he will be glorious in his saints, that maketh us rejoice. We shall see all our friends in heaven. There we shall see the excellency of the happiness of Christ, his love, his grace, his mercy.

The words are expressed with a kind of glorying, 'Lo, this is our God.' So that the joy of a Christian endeth in glory, and in the highest degree of glory, as you have it, Rom. 5:3, 'We glory also in tribulation, we glory in hope of glory,' nay, we glory in God as ours reconciled. And if we glory in him now as a God reconciled, what shall we do in heaven? Can a worldling glory in his riches, his greatness, his favour from such a man, as Haman did? And shall not a Christian glory in his God? and make his boast in his God? And therefore in this world we should learn to glory, before we come to that glory in heaven, specially when we be set upon by anything that is apt to discourage us. Glory then in our Head. Perhaps a Christian hath no wealth, no great rents to glory in, aye, but he hath a God to glory in, let him glory in him. The world may take all else from him, but not his God. As the church, in Song of Sol. 5. The virgins put the church to describe her beloved, 'What is thy beloved more than another beloved? My beloved is white and ruddy, the chiefest of ten thousand.' Then she goeth on in particulars, 'my beloved is thus and thus'; and if you would know what my beloved is, 'this is my beloved.' So a Christian that hath a spirit of faith should glory in God here, for heaven is begun here, and he should glory in Christ his Saviour, and should set Christ against all discouragements and oppositions. If you will know what is my beloved, 'this is my beloved, the chief among ten thousands.' Psa. 115:3. 'Our God is in heaven, and doth whatsoever he pleaseth, in heaven, and earth, and the deeps,' yea, we make our boast of God, saith the psalmist, when there is occasion. 'This is the Lord, this is our God; we have waited for him,' specially in times of afflictions; and what is the reason? This will hold out to eternity. 'This is our God.' As in the Revelations, it is a plea, and a glory forever; for God is our happiness. As the schoolmen say, he is our objective happiness, and our formal happiness; he is our happiness, as he is ours, and he is ours in life and death, and forever. So there is always ground of glory, only God doth discover himself to be ours by little and little, as we are able to bear him. He is ours in our worst times. 'My God, my God, why hast thou forsaken me?' Yet my God still, Matt. 27:46.

He is our God to death, and he is ours in heaven. 'This is our God; we will rejoice in him.' And therefore well may we boast of God, because in God is everlasting salvation. If we boasted in anything else, our boasting would determine with the thing itself; but if we rejoice in God, we rejoice in that which is of equal continuance with our souls, and goeth along with the soul to all eternity.

And therefore we should learn to rejoice in God, and then we shall never be ashamed. It is spoken here with a kind of exalting, a kind of triumphing over all oppositions, 'Lo, this is our God.' Beloved, this, that God is our God, and Christ is ours, is the ground of rejoicing, and of all happiness. All joy, all comfort is founded upon this our interest in God; and therefore,

1. We must make this good *while we live here, that God is our God*, and that we may do so, observe this. Christ is called *Emmanuel*, God with us. God, in the second person, is God-man, and so God with us, and the Father in Emmanuel is God with us too. So we are God the Father's, because we are his. 'All things are yours,' saith the apostle, 'whether Paul or Apollos, things present, things to come.' 'Why?' 'Because you are Christ's,' 1 Cor. 3:22. Aye, but what if I be Christ's, Christ is God's? So we must be Christ's, and then

we shall be God's. If Christ be ours, God is ours, for God is Emmanuel, in Christ, Emmanuel, God is with us in Christ, who is with us. God is reconciled to us in God and man, in our nature; and therefore get by faith into Christ, and get union, and get communion; by prayer open our souls to him, entertain his speeches to us by his word and Spirit and blessed motions, and open our spirits to him, and so maintain a blessed intercourse.

2. Make it good that God is our God by daily acquaintance. These speeches at the latter end are founded upon acquaintance before. 'This is our God.' Grace and glory are knit together indissolubly. If God be our God here, he will be ours also in glory; if not here, not in glory. There is a communion with God here, before communion with him in glory, and therefore make it good that God be our God here first, by union with him. And then maintain daily acquaintance with him, by seeing him with the eye of faith, by speaking to him, and hearing him speak to us by his Spirit, joining in his ordinances, and then he will own us, and be acquainted with us. In heaven we shall say, 'Lo, this is our God.' We have had sweet acquaintance one with another: he by his Spirit with me, and I by my prayers with him. Our Saviour Christ will not be without us in heaven. We are part of his mystical body, and heaven were not heaven to Christ without us. With reverence be it spoken, we are the fulness of Christ, as he is the fulness of his church. And if he should want us, in some sort he were miserable, he having fixed upon us as objects of his eternal love. In what case were he if he should lose that object? And therefore, as we glory in him, he glorieth in us. 'Who is this that cometh out of the wilderness?' 'Who?' 'His beloved,'

Song of Sol. 3:6. And, 'Woman, is this thy faith?' Matt. 15:28.
He admires the graces of the church, as the church admires
him. 'This is the Lord.' The church cannot be without him,
nor he without the church. These words are spoken with a
kind of admiration. 'Lo, this is the Lord, we will rejoice in
him.' So I say, as there is thanks and joy, so there is admiration, 'Lo, behold!' This is a God worthy beholding, and so
he wonders at the graces of his children. Beloved, there is
nothing in the world worthy admiration. *Sapientis non est
admirari.* It was a speech of the proud philosopher, a wise
man will not admire, for he knoweth the ground.[1] But in
heaven the parts are lifted up so high that there is nothing
but matter of admiration, things 'that eye hath not seen,
nor ear heard, nor hath entered into the heart of man to
conceive of,' 1 Cor. 2:9. They be things beyond expression,
and nothing is fit for them but admiration at the great
things vouchsafed to the church.

And as with admiration, so with invitation. That is the
nature of true thankfulness. There is no envy in spiritual
things. No man envieth another the light of the Scriptures,
but lo, behold with admiration and invitation of all others,
'This is the Lord.'

Let us therefore rejoice beforehand, at the glorious times
to come, both to ourselves and to others; be stirring and
exciting one another to glory, and rejoice in God our salvation.

1. And, therefore, learn all to be stirred up from hence,
not to be offended with Christ, or with religion. Be not

---

[1] 'A wise man will not admire,' i.e., wonder. Cf. Horace, Epist.
I.vi.1. The maxim is ascribed to Democritus.

offended, saith Augustine, with the parvity[1] of religion. Everything to the eyes of the world is little in religion. A Christian is a despised person, and the church, the meanest part of the world, in regard to outward glory. But,

2. Consider with the littleness, and baseness, and despisedness of the church, *the glory to come*. Time will come when we shall rejoice, and not only see, but boast with admiration, to the stirring up of others, 'Lo, this is the Lord.' And, therefore, say with our Saviour Christ, 'happy is he that is not offended with me,' Matt. 11:6, nor with religion. There is a time coming, that will make amends for all. Who in the world can say at the hour of death, and day of judgment, Lo, this is my riches, this my honours! Alas! the greatest persons must stand naked to give account; all must stand on even ground to hold up their hands at the great bar. We may say to the carnal presumptuous man, Lo, this is the man that put his confidence in his riches. And none but reconciled Christians can say, 'Lo, this is our God.' Therefore take heed of being offended with anything in religion.

3. Again, if time to come be so transcendently glorious, *let us not be afraid to die*, let us not be overmuch cast down, for it shall end in glory. And let us be in expectation still of good times, wait for this blessed time to come, and never be content with any condition, so as to set up our rest here. We may write upon everything, *hic non est requies vestra*.[2] Our rest is behind; these things are in passage. And therefore rest content with nothing here. Heaven is our centre,

[1] That is, 'insignificance, smallness.'
[2] Latin: 'this is not the place for your rest.'

our element, our happiness; and everything is contentedly happy, and thriveth in its element. The birds in the air, the fish in the sea, beasts on the earth, they rest there as in their centre. And that that is our place forever, it is heaven, it is God. The immediate enjoying of God in heaven, that is our rest, our element, and we shall never rest till we be there. And therefore he is befooled for it, in the gospel, that setteth up his rest here. Whosoever saith I have enough, and will now take contentment in them, he is a fool. 'There is a rest for God's people,' Heb. 4:9, but it is not here.

4. Neither *rest in any measure of grace, or comfort.* What is faith to sight? We have hope, an anchor, and helmet, that keepeth up many a soul, as the cork keepeth from sinking. What is this hope to the fruition of what we hope for? Here we have love, many love tokens from God. Aye, but what is love to union? Ours is but a love of desire. We are but in motion here, we lie in motion only; and our desires are not accomplished. What is this love to the accomplishing of the union with the thing beloved forever? Here we have communion of saints. But what is this communion of saints to communion with God forever? We have infirmities here, as others, which breedeth jealousies and suspicion. Aye, but we shall have communion in heaven, and there shall be nothing in us to distaste others, but everlasting friendship. Yea, our communion shall be with perfect souls. Our communion of saints here is our heaven upon earth, but it is communion with unperfect souls. Peace we have, aye, but it is peace intermixed, it is peace in the midst of enemies. There we shall have peace without enemies. Christ doth now rule in the midst of enemies. In heaven he shall

rule in the midst of his friends. So that we can imagine no condition here, though never so good, but it is imperfect. And therefore rest not in anything in the world, no not in any measure of grace, any measure of comfort, till we be in heaven, but wait for the time to come, 'and rejoice in hope by which we are saved,' Rom. 12:12. Wait still, and though we have not content here, yet this is not our home, this is a good refreshment by the way. As when the children of Israel came from Babylon, they had wells by the way, as in *Michae*,[1] they digged up wells. So from Babylon to Jerusalem we have many sweet refreshments; but they be refreshments far off the way. God digs many wells; we have breasts of consolation to comfort us, aye, but they are but for the way. And therefore let us answer all temptations, and not take contentment with anything here. It is good, but it is not our home. *Cui dulcis peregrinatio, non amat patriam.*[2] If we have[3] eternity, love heaven, we cannot be overmuch taken with anything in the way.

5. And so for the church, *let us not be overmuch dejected for the desolation of the church*, but pray for a spirit of faith, which doth realise things to the soul and presents them as present to the soul, seeth Babylon fallen, presents things in the Scripture phrase, and in the words, 'Babylon is fallen,' forasmuch as all the enemies of the church fall. Mighty is the Lord that hath spoken, and will perform it, and, as the angel saith, 'it is done,' Rev. 16:17. So time will come ere long

[1] Sic ... But qu. 'Micah' and the reference, Micha 1:4? Or 'Baca'? Psa. 84:6.

[2] Latin: 'Anyone who finds pleasure in journeying in a foreign country does not love his own native land.'

[3] Qu. 'love'?

when it shall be said, 'It is done.' The church shall be gathered, and then, 'Lo, this is our God.'

It was the comfort of the believing Jews that the Gentiles should come. And why should it not be the comfort of the Gentiles that there be blessed times for the ancient people of God, when they shall all cry and say, 'Lo, this is our God; we have waited for him long, and he will save us.' Therefore, be not overmuch discouraged for whatsoever present desolation the church lieth under. If it were not for this, 'we were of all men most miserable,' as Paul saith, 1 Cor. 15:19. But there be times to come when we shall rejoice, and rejoice forever, and make boast of the Lord. If it were not, 'we were of all men most miserable.' Howsoever happiness is to come, yet of all persons he is most happy that hath Christ and heaven. The very foretaste of happiness is worth all the world. The inward peace of conscience, joy in the Holy Ghost, the beginnings of the image of God and of happiness here, is worth all the enjoyments of the world. Ask of any Christian whether he will hang with the greatest worldling, and be in his condition; he would not change his place in grace for all his glory. And therefore, set heaven aside, the very first-fruits is better than all the harvest of the world. Let us therefore get the soul raised by faith to see her happiness. We need it all, for till the soul get a frame raised up to see its happiness here, specially in the world to come, it is not in a frame fit for any service, it will stoop to any base sin. Where the affections are so possessed, they look upon all base courses as unworthy of their hope. What! I that hope to rejoice forever with God in heaven, that am heir of heaven, that have the image of God upon me, that am in covenant with God, to take any bestial course, to place my happiness in things meaner than myself, that have God to delight in, a God in covenant, that hath taken me into covenant with himself. So I say in all solicitations to sin, get ourselves into a frame that may stand firm and immoveable.

In all troubles let us know we have a God in covenant, that we may joy in him here, and rejoice with him in heaven forever hereafter.

―――――